DESIGNING

E-Learning

Here Is How You Can

- Adapt Your ISD Skills to E-Learning

- Blend Solutions to Ensure
  Learning Sticks

- Make Effective Design Choices

ASTD

*Linking People,
Learning & Performance*

D1469020

Saul Carliner

Ordering information: Books published by ASTD can be ordered by calling 800.628.2783 or 703.683.8100, or via the Website at www.astd.org.

Library of Congress Catalog Card Number: 2002105495

ISBN: 1-56286-332-0

Contents

Preface

WHAT IS THIS BOOK ABOUT?

This book is the fifth in ASTD's e-learning series. Although instructional design for e-learning has much in common with design for traditional training, there are many important differences. Instructional design—whether for traditional, stand-up classroom training or for e-learning—is largely a problem-solving process.

Within the context of the design process, I present the many choices you face, describe different learning issues, and present available approaches for e-learning. I also describe the issues you should consider as you narrow the range of options for your e-learning design. The solution you ultimately choose must balance the educational needs of learners, the practical constraints under which your project operates, and your own preferences and experiences.

The creativity involved in framing the problem, making these choices, and implementing them is what initially drew me to the field of instructional design. But, to a novice, the many choices and myriad options available for each choice can seem overwhelming at first. The number of choices for traditional training programs is extensive; moving them online only adds to the number.

Although some software claims to simplify and shorten the design process, the truth is that structured, clear thinking takes time. In fact, because the process is unfamiliar to many first-time designers and developers of online learning programs, experts caution that a first course may take twice as long to design and develop as one designed and developed by a team experienced with e-learning.

Although the instructional system design (ISD) process for e-learning can be complex, I have simplified each step in the process by identifying the choices available and the key issues to consider as you make those choices. These issues are described in plain language, only using technical terminology when necessary and defining it on the first use. In some instances, however, I introduce a basic framework for approaching a design decision; other books in this series cover the material in more depth. For example, I introduce the issues and type of evaluations where they arise in the design process, and leave it to William Horton to explain how to create meaningful evaluations in his book *Evaluating E-Learning* (ASTD, 2001).

WHO SHOULD READ THIS BOOK?

Instructional designers, course developers, managers, trainers, information designers (architects), performance technologists, and technical communicators preparing to work on their first or second e-learning courses will find this book helpful.

When writing this book, I assumed that most of you will be designing and developing asynchronous courses—courses in which learners and instructors are separated by time and location. Certainly the material presented here applies to synchronous e-learning—where learners and instructors are online at the same time—but that's not the primary use.

HOW TO USE THIS BOOK

Designing E-Learning is divided into five sections. The first section is dedicated to introductory material with some valuable advice about how you can transfer your repertoire of ISD skills to the world of e-learning. Each of the remaining sections covers the four phases of ISD for e-learning:

- definition phase
- e-learning design phase
- e-learning development phase
- production and maintenance phase.

Like the other books in the e-learning series, each chapter of this book ends with a "Your Turn" section that allows you to apply the concepts learned in the book. These exercises will help you think through the points made in the chapter and apply them directly to your e-learning project.

Less-experienced designers and developers of online learning programs will likely benefit most by working their way through this book from front to back. Designers and developers who have more experience may wish to glance at the "Your Turn" section at the end of each chapter to evaluate their knowledge of the material covered in that chapter. That way, they can identify their knowledge gaps quickly and concentrate on those areas.

ACKNOWLEDGMENTS

I would like to thank Phil Jones, Sarah Boehle, Steve Dahlberg, Julie Groshens, Marc Hequet, and Leah Nelson at VNU Business Media for their support and encouragement of my work in e-learning, and Francis "Skip" Atkinson, Bryan Chapman, Margaret Driscoll, Gloria Gery, George Hayhoe, Craig Marion, Whitney Quesenbery, and Patti Shank for brainstorming and clarifying ideas with me. In addition to the works cited, these ideas resulting from these interactions form the kernel of this book.

I would also like to thank the following people and organizations for providing screenshots used in this book: Kathy Blake of Bentley College; Greg Brower and David Posner of Cisco; Whitney Quesenbery of Cognetics; Greg Stevens of Home Depot; Tao Le and Allen Levinson of Medsn.com; Chris Maxwell of Ojalá, Inc.; Clark Aldrich of SimuLearn; Debbie Smigocki of Verity; Stephen Walsh of XHLP; the VNU Business Team; and Bethany Bishop, Cesira Daukantis, and my Advanced Content Development class of spring 2002.

LOOKING AHEAD

When you finish reading this book, I hope that you not only feel comfortable about working on e-learning projects but enthusiastic about them. For those of us who are always looking for new ideas and new approaches to training, e-learning provides that and more; it provides a new frontier to explore.

Saul Carliner
September 2002

1

Designing E-Learning: Considering the Possibilities

UNDERSTANDING E-LEARNING

Welcome to your first e-learning project. As you begin, you face a number of challenges. First is working past the myths about e-learning. Some advocates claim it is more effective than the classroom. Some even claim it will replace the classroom. Neither is true. Studies suggest that e-learning is as effective as classroom learning—no more, no less—but teaches more efficiently. Learning time can be reduced by as much as a third, often more. And, as the e-learning movement grows, experts agree that e-learning works best when it is blended with classroom learning.

The second challenge is mastering a slightly different instructional design process. Although many of the general activities are the same as those used for designing materials for workbooks or classrooms, some of the specific activities are different.

The last challenge is that of working with a new medium of communication. E-learning challenges people who are experienced at developing classroom courses or workbooks to develop a new repertoire of teaching strategies for the computer. In some ways, the computer seems more restrictive than the more familiar classroom or page. In other ways, it opens up new and exciting possibilities for learning.

Before starting your first e-learning project, you should first learn about these possibilities. That's the purpose of this chapter. It describes the possibilities for e-learning by first introducing the different types of e-learning. When doing so, it explains how you can use e-learning for both formal and informal learning. Then, this chapter presents some of the issues that arise as you consider the use of these different types of e-learning in your organization. Finally, it explores how you can blend different types of e-learning with classroom learning to transfer learning back to the job—and improve the performance of workers and your organization.

Portions of this chapter adapted with permission of VNU Business Media from *An Overview of Online Learning,* by S. Carliner. (1999). Amherst, MA: HRD Press.

CROSSING THE CLASSROOM BOUNDARIES

Because the primary package for training in the classroom is the course, trainers naturally gravitate to the idea of packaging learning material online as courses. In fact, the processes and systems of most training departments are designed for use with courses. It's the unit in which trainers deliver content. It's the primary deliverable that results from trainers' efforts. For many training organizations, it's the unit of billing for services. And, it's the unit for measuring effectiveness; that is, most training departments assess the effectiveness of their work by assessing the effectiveness of their courses.

Classroom courses represent a type of learning called *formal learning* because the learning has stated objectives and is supposed to yield predetermined results. Some forms of e-learning—online education and online training—re-create the formal learning experience online.

Other forms of e-learning move beyond formal learning to provide learning when, where, and how learners need it. Such learning does not have stated objectives because each learner has a different goal, yet many can achieve their goals using the same learning material. This type of learning is called *informal* because it does not identify outcomes that learners should achieve. Learners set their own learning. Two forms of e-learning—knowledge management and electronic performance support—qualify as informal learning methods.

The next several sections describe the four main types of online learning: online education, online training, knowledge management, and electronic performance support. In addition, blended learning—a combination of e-learning and traditional learning systems—is another option that can fall under the category of formal or informal learning. Table 1-1 represents a model showing the relationships among these different uses of e-learning.

Table 1-1. The uses of e-learning.

Formal Learning	Informal Learning
• Online education • Online training • Blended learning with classroom delivery and printed materials	• Knowledge management • Electronic performance support • Blended learning with related materials in other media

FORMAL LEARNING ONLINE

Formal learning is intentional. The learning materials begin with specific objectives that have been identified by the course developer in conjunction with the sponsors and subject matter experts. Learning is assessed by the extent to which learners achieve those objectives. This type of learning may put the trainer in the position of a "control freak" who feels a need to control what learners do learn and measure his or her own performance by the extent to which the learners do so. Formal learning online takes two forms: online education and online training.

Learning Through Online Education

What Is Online Education? Education is a structured event specifically intended to develop durable knowledge and skills. When the event occurs in a classroom, the instructor is a person. When the event occurs online, the computer becomes the instructor. At least two types of education are considered to be online: synchronous and asynchronous learning.

Synchronous Online Instruction. Online classrooms are classroom-like events in which students and instructors are separated by geography but working together at the same time. Because the instructor and learners are online at the same time, the instruction is called synchronous.

At the least, instructors and students interact with one another by "chatting" online—typing in messages that all of the people who are connected to the event can see. The chat might be a formal one, in which an instructor "lectures" first and an online conversation follows.

At the most, the event includes an Internet broadcast of the instructor, a simultaneous presentation of a related visual, perhaps a whiteboard on which instructors can write notes much like on a blackboard to be viewed by all participants. Students respond with oral or written questions.

Asynchronous Online Instruction. Online education also refers to a structured learning experience presented on a computer and in which the instructor and learner are separated by both time and geography. Because learners and instructors do not need to be online at the same time, this type of online training and education is called asynchronous.

Materials are organized into courses and include a combination of formal teaching sequences and exercises, such as problems to solve and simulations to experience.

Individual learners directly interact with the computer to proceed through the courses. Ideally, these courses engage students through meaningful interaction and let students direct their own learning. These courses often include assessments or testing.

Both Types of Instruction. Participants usually take these courses in the academic style: a few hours a week over a period of several weeks or months (both synchronous and asynchronous courses). Between class sessions, participants usually have homework assignments, such as assigned readings, papers, and even group assignments.

To facilitate a sense of community outside of the regularly scheduled synchronous classes and for those who take courses asynchronously, many instructors facilitate ongoing discussion lists outside. Participants contribute to the discussion outside of class.

Many online courses also have extensive resources online, including the following:

- textbooks, which can be created by assembling readings from a variety of sources and instructor's notes into a single text
- supplementary readings
- remediation (that is, an alternative presentation of course content that helps learners who did not master the material on the first try)
- enrichment exercises
- worksheets
- interesting links.

How Are Organizations Using Online Education? Uses of online education are as varied as organizations using this type of learning. Consider these varied educational uses:

- *Basic skills training:* Online education provides adults with limited literacy skills with a safe, patient place to develop those skills. Some of the courses are adapted from similar programs that teach children basic reading and mathematics skills, and others are developed specifically for adults.
- *Online degrees:* Established universities offer individual courses, certificate programs, and degree programs online. For example, San Diego State University offers a certificate in educational technology online.
- *Management education:* Some major corporations conduct part of their management education online. Participants are assigned to work groups who "meet" online a few hours per week for the several weeks preceding a classroom course. During their online collaboration, participants first read policies and background material and then work through cases of actual management problems.

Learning Through Online Training

What Is Online Training? Like online education, training is a structured event specifically intended to develop knowledge and skills. What separates training from education, however, is that the skills and knowledge taught via training are expected to be used immediately.

The forms of online training are similar to that of online education: synchronous Webcasts and asynchronous courses.

Unlike online education, learners usually take online training courses start-to-finish with minimal interruption and rarely have homework between classes. For example, a learner might take an online training course in a single two-hour session. Because the skills taught might be needed at any time, online training courses are usually asynchronous, so learners can take them whenever they need them. In fact, online training courses are often called just-in-time training because of their anytime, anywhere availability.

To provide online learners with a sense of community and a feeling that their learning is not anonymous, some organizations also provide online discussion groups for courses, so learners can interact with one another. Similarly, some organizations provide e-coaching services, so learners have someone to contact if they have questions or need tutoring on challenging course material.

Because online training courses have explicitly stated objectives and often have tests to assess whether students mastered them, the learning is considered to be formal.

How Are Organizations Using Online Training? Uses of online training are as varied as organizations using this type of learning. Consider these uses:

- teaching the use of common business applications, such as WordPerfect, Microsoft Access, and Lotus 1-2-3
- teaching quality control, especially topics like statistical process control

Technology Needed for Online Education and Training

For developing synchronous courses:
- network
- database program
- well-designed database that uses terms and categories familiar to all users
- groupware (programs that encourage people to share information)

For developing asynchronous courses:
- computer with the capability of working with large graphics and video files
- word processor for preparing the text of the learning program
- authoring tools (software for creating course interactive material), such as Blackboard, Click2Learn's Toolbook, Macromedia DreamWeaver CourseBuilder
- presentation software for preparing slides and visuals, if any, such as Microsoft PowerPoint or Macromedia Flash
- software for retouching photos, such as Adobe PhotoShop

For delivering asynchronous courses to learners:
- computer
- software for viewing the course material
- sound card and speakers (if sound is used)
- software for playing the course material
- software for playing audio clips
- software for playing video sequences

- placing routine, technical aspects of employee orientation online
- providing training required by regulators, such as an annual refresher course on the procedures used to protect information within the company from inappropriate and unauthorized use.
- offering professional development skills training, such as that shown in figure 1-1.

INFORMAL LEARNING ONLINE

Although formal learning is often necessary in the workplace, just as frequently people learn without the direction of learning professionals. Learners identify what

---

Figure 1-1. Example of online education.

This Virtual Leader course helps learners develop leadership skills by placing them in a simulation of a business meeting with conflict.

Source: Reprinted with permission from SimuLearn. 2002.

they need to learn, determine where the content exists, and continue to work on their learning until they master the topic. In other instances, people learn unintentionally. They serendipitously encounter useful content that they choose to retain.

This type of learning is called informal learning because it does not begin with objectives that were initially established by the learning professionals, it occurs at the instigation of learners (rather than the requirement by management or with the anticipation of any outside recognition), and its measures of effectiveness vary with the needs of the learners.

Although the classroom primarily limits learning professionals to formal learning, e-learning allows them to explore the potential of informal learning. Informal learning online takes two forms: knowledge management and electronic performance support.

Learning Through Knowledge Management

What Is Knowledge Management? Knowledge management is capturing, storing, transforming, and disseminating information within an organization, with the goal of promoting efficiency at the least and innovation and competitive advantage at the most. More specifically, the goal of knowledge management is to provide access to the following types of information to all who need to know:

- formal corporate information such as policies, procedures, and product information
- informal information, such as documents, reports, presentations, and proposals
- expertise, often recorded in documents like lessons learned, stories, and case histories, but also available through direct online interaction with colleagues.

The recorded information is stored in a special database called a knowledge base. Because the knowledge base is a large reference, it is sometimes called an online reference. Because users have access to information—and the resultant learning— whenever they need it, knowledge management promotes just-in-time learning. People interact with the knowledge base when they need information from it. Learning occurs by interacting with the database in ways that are meaningful to the users, much as learning occurs from an encyclopedia in ways that are meaningful to the users.

Knowledge management can also include online chats, discussions, and symposia, during which participants can exchange tacit knowledge—content that exists within an individual or organization but has not yet been recorded or exchanged.

How Are Organizations Using Knowledge Management? Many of the pivotal developments in knowledge management come from the information systems (IS) community. Thomas Davenport and Lawrence Prusack, for example, have written a number of books about the value to be mined from corporate information (Davenport & Prusack, 1997; Prusack, 1997).

Consulting firms have been leaders in applying knowledge management. Although each of the clients served by these firms has unique needs, the problems they face are similar. When consulting firms find similarities, they can leverage previous work such as proposals, work plans, programs, and other materials prepared for clients facing similar challenges. The consultant can reuse the effective elements of these materials, adapt the materials when a client situation warrants, and change those elements of the materials that didn't work in the first client's environment to avoid repeating mistakes.

These knowledge bases often include lessons learned in a particular situation and provide contact information so that a consultant on a second account can get more information about the earlier experience. To make sure that employees contribute to the company knowledge base, some consulting firms assess employees' contributions as part of the performance appraisal process.

Figure 1-2 shows an example of a homepage from a corporate knowledge base.

Learning Through Electronic Performance Support

What Is Electronic Performance Support? Electronic performance support refers to a work environment on a computer in which performers receive assistance with tasks or in completing work. For example, with the help of performance support, a customer

Figure 1-2. The homepage for George, a knowledge management system used internally within a company to share basic information (like telephone numbers) and complex information (like project information).

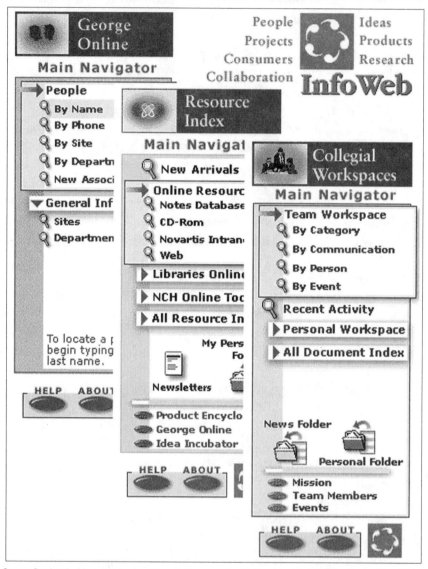

Source: Reprinted with permission from Novartis Consumer Health. Developed by Cognetics Corporation. 2000.

service representative at an "e-tailer" might be prompted to ask if a customer wants to purchase the matching scarf when buying a knit hat.

The software that provides performance support is often called an electronic performance support system (EPSS). An EPSS provides the information, training, coaching, and monitoring needed for such performance. In some instances, the EPSS even handles tasks for workers. They're part online help, part online tutorial, part database, part application program, and part expert system. They can be separate programs or included as part of existing programs.

In a learning context that's focused on performance support, performance—not competence—is the goal. If the system can perform the task for users, then the system does so and users learn to do; they need not learn the *why* and *what* underlying the *how.*

Learning is, therefore, coincidental, and performers may or may not develop specific skills and achieve domain learning. Because the learner is not directly connected to a live instructor or coach when performance is supported, the learning is asynchronous.

How Are Organizations Using Electronic Performance Support? Organizations are using EPSSs in almost every aspect of corporate life. Consider this example from customer service: A customer calls, asking for an increased credit limit. After requesting an account number and security information, the customer service representative views the caller's record on the computer. The representative asks the computer to evaluate the caller's credit history, recommend whether an increase is appropriate and, if so, the extent of the increase.

In this situation, electronic performance support lets a relatively inexperienced customer service representative perform work that in the past had been performed by a more experienced and specialized credit analyst.

Consider this example from the field of medicine. One of the most significant problems with prescribing medicine is how one medicine reacts with another. But, knowing the effects isn't easy; experts estimate that keeping up with new developments in drugs would require that doctors spend eight hours a week reading about medicine.

> ### Technology Needed for Electronic Performance Support
>
> **For preparing informative text:**
> - word processor
> - course authoring tools
> - help authoring tools
> - hypertext markup language (HTML) authoring tools (or other tools for preparing information to be read online)
>
> **For monitoring work performance:**
> - programming language
> - monitoring software
>
> **For automating tasks:**
> - programming language
> - course authoring tools
> - HTML authoring tools
> - connection to a network (optional)

Because that's impossible, an EPSS was developed. Doctors can enter a patient's medical history into the system, list the drugs currently taken, and name the ones they would also like to prescribe. The system responds with a list of potential interactions. Based on this information, doctors can determine whether or not to prescribe a given medicine to a patient.

In this situation, an EPSS helps an expert make a better-informed decision than would be possible without the system.

CONSIDER THE MEDIUM WHEN DESIGNING E-LEARNING PRODUCTS

Imagine that you have just read a novel and are watching its adaptation to the screen. You might like both versions of the story, but the two are different. Most likely, the novel contains more detail, more of the back story. In the novel, the author takes as much as a page to describe the setting that the director of the film establishes in a five-second shot. In some cases, a story that reads well on the page transfers poorly to the screen. In other cases, both versions work well but the creators of the two versions tell the story differently.

The types of online learning just described represent four different approaches to teaching content. The first two—online education and training—resemble approaches widely used in the classroom. The other two—knowledge management and electronic performance support—represent new ways of conveying material to learners.

As novelists must adapt their writing techniques when converting their printed works to screenplays, so training and human performance improvement (HPI) professionals must adjust their teaching techniques when preparing content for online presentation. In fact, because much of online learning looks different than what is seen in the classroom, many situations challenge learning professional to adapt not only their techniques, but also what they value as important when designing online learning products.

One of the first adaptations is the transition from a completely formal training library to one that includes both formal and informal learning products.

Adapting Design Techniques for Formal Learning

Formal learning online resembles its classroom counterpart in many ways. Like classroom training, formal online learning also has stated learning objectives. It challenges the learning professional to create an interactive and supportive learning environment, use tests and other types of assessments to evaluate learning, and keep extensive, complete records. Learners only receive credit for a formal learning experience if they complete the course and pass a test (or some similar type of learning assessment).

Computers simplify testing and record keeping, but they complicate other parts of this effort. For example, instructional designers must make sure that learners have the necessary software on their computers and that the courses run without errors. Even if these parts work, the connections with computers can fail while the student is supposed to be taking the course. Or, students can "cheat" by pretending to be other students.

A more significant complication, however, is that computers are impersonal devices. With self-enrollment and without a classroom, learning online can easily become an anonymous experience. That anonymity demotivates learners.

Interactivity, already a challenge in the classroom, becomes a more significant challenge online. Conversations that instructors can easily initiate in the classroom become impossible in asynchronous classrooms. Interactive simulations and exercises—popular forms of interaction with learners—often require complex programming to appear fully engaging.

So many designers of online instruction rely heavily on text. More than the dreariness of turning endless pages of text (perhaps mixed with some ornamental clip art), this approach creates a significant learning problem because reading online is less accurate than in print. Typically, readers online read more slowly than in print. Readers also comprehend less (and with more errors) because they skim text rather than read it (Price & Price, 2002). Designers must address these realities when presenting information.

Adapting Design Techniques for Informal Learning

Although some online learning is formal, much more is informal. Informal learning often does not have stated learning outcomes. It is available when learners need it. It usually does not require an official enrollment process, so completions are not recorded. Although it sometimes encompasses learning of explicit information (knowledge that can be recorded), it also encompasses tacit information (knowledge that is not easily recorded, because the people who possess it are not consciously aware of it).

Designing informal learning presents a significant challenge to training and HPI professionals. Because formal training and most organizational processes mandate that every training program have stated objectives and evaluation, the lack of these requires a shift in thinking (Carliner, 1995). Rather than developing objectives that all learners must achieve, the design process begins by preparing objectives that learners who choose to complete the content should achieve.

Informal learning is self-directed; that is, learners guide and motivate themselves through the learning effort. In some cases, that means that learners have a clear goal in mind and leave the learning experience before completing the objectives. In such instances, organizations need to determine whether they believe that learners have actually completed their work. No consensus exists yet within the training and HPI community on this point.

Informal learners are also time-bound; that is, they want to learn as much information in as little time as possible. Interactivity and exercises that engage learners in formal courses often annoy time-pressured learners of informal learning products, who just want to get to the point and get out. In such instances, efforts to infuse interactivity into the learning products are often focused on creating the fastest path to the information through specialized searches and tight links.

Because informal learning often happens without any involvement from the learning staff, the learning materials must completely communicate ideas on their own. Training and HPI professionals must ensure the clarity of the terminology and content, because learners cannot ask questions easily. Similarly, without body expressions to read, training and HPI professionals must make sure that their content supports the learner without sending unintended messages that could interfere with the learning process.

Informal learning also creates challenges in record keeping and evaluation of online learning products. Because learners often do not register for informal learning opportunities, no formal records exist. Instead, training and HPI professionals must rely on other types of records, such as the count of the number of visits to particular Webpages. Such counts are impossible with CD-ROM and digital versatile disc (DVD) technologies.

Similarly, because informal learners each have their own agendas and often learn only as much as needed to achieve their immediate goals, testing is usually an ineffective and inappropriate means of assessing the effectiveness of learning products. Furthermore, because many informal learners might spend five minutes or less with an informal learning product, they are not likely to complete a "smiley face" evaluation.

In other words, the Kirkpatrick (1998) model of evaluation, which offers four levels of evaluating a training course—reaction, learning, behavior, and results— and is widely used among training and HPI groups, does not apply to informal online learning.

BLENDING DIFFERENT TYPES OF LEARNING

Although some people express concern that e-learning might spell the end of classroom training or that it is inferior to classroom training, e-learning ultimately will complement it. Training and HPI professionals use classroom training for what it does best and do likewise for e-learning.

E-learning is outstanding for teaching rote skills; it has the infinite patience needed to do so. With the privacy of the computer, slower learners can have the extensive remediation they need, and fast learners can speed through a course, unencumbered by their classmates.

E-learning is also an excellent tool for teaching prerequisite material. Instructors can require learners to take a prerequisite course and pass a pre-class test before coming to the classroom. In that way, the instructor can begin the classroom course at a higher level, sure that each learner has completed the prerequisite learning. As a result, the classroom course can provide an in-depth learning experience, a shorter learning experience, or both.

In contrast, the classroom provides an opportunity to develop higher-order thinking skills and simulate interpersonal exchanges. Although these can be accomplished online through simulations and synchronous learning, they often have more impact with learners in the classroom.

In some cases, e-learning can complement a classroom course or vice versa. For example, because instructors must focus classroom courses on the typical learner, they can rarely meet the needs of individual learners. Instructors can develop course

Websites with remedial material, providing slow learners with additional opportunities to master the content. For learners who need to adapt the material to specific needs or want to continue with the material, instructors can use a Website for enrichment material.

Similarly, some online learners have difficulty with the material, even though it might have been extensively tested with prospective learners. Others need gentle reminders to motivate them to complete courses. In such cases, personal coaching provides assistance. The coach is a person with whom the learner interacts. In some cases, the coach is available in person, in others, online or by telephone.

When a learning product involves a combination of classroom and online components, the learning is said to be blended (Mantyla, 2001). Ultimately, blending classroom and e-learning, and formal and informal learning can help learners transfer the new skills to the job.

Ultimately, the mission of HPI professionals is to improve learners' on-the-job performance. More than merely teaching learners what to do, their job involves making sure learners use those skills on the job so organizations realize the improved business results that drove them to invest in the learning program.

To make this happen, a typical e-learning program ideally encompasses more than an isolated learning product. Rather, it encompasses a series of related learning products that together create a campaign for improved performance. Some of these products—demonstrations and marketing materials, in particular—are intended to introduce a topic and inspire interest among prospective learners.

Some learning products teach people how to perform new skills and assess their mastery of them. Typically, these are formal learning products such as classroom and online courses.

Some learning products are intended to help people apply the skills back on-the-job and extend their use of the skills. Frequently, these are informal learning products such as job aids, coaches (software that monitors performance and provides feedback), reference material, and databases with answers to questions not raised in the course. Chapter 5 offers more concrete assistance in choosing the components of a performance improvement campaign.

YOUR TURN

This chapter introduced you to the possibilities of e-learning. It described the two categories of learning—formal and informal—and the four types of e-learning—online education, online training, knowledge management, and performance support. It also explained some of the similarities and differences between classroom and online learning. Now, using worksheet 1-1, apply these lessons as you continue or begin to develop your own e-learning products.

For more information about these different types of e-learning and links to additional examples, please visit the companion Website: http://saulcarliner.home.att.net /oll/index.html.

Worksheet 1-1. Plan your own e-learning courses.

When choosing to develop e-learning, what types of learning products can you create?

For formal learning?	For informal learning?

As you approach an e-learning project, what implications and types of learning should you consider?

List hardware and software improvements and additions that will be necessary to implement your e-learning project:

List some opportunities in your organization for blending e-learning with more traditional training forms:

2

Adapting ISD for E-Learning

The most challenging aspect of any online learning project, especially a first one, is where to begin. The framework for understanding a learning problem, defining it, making design choices, and committing to those choices is called the instructional system design (ISD) process. It is widely followed in classroom instruction and becomes even more critical to e-learning projects.

This chapter introduces the ISD process. It first describes the role of a process in ensuring that instructional issues are each addressed at appropriate times. Next, it names the key phases in the process for designing an online learning program. Then, it describes how to achieve efficiencies in the process (and when you should not expect efficiency). Last, this chapter describes the limitations of a process.

ABOUT THE ISD PROCESS

One of the most perplexing questions about design is, what is it? Some believe it is a science, guided by the results of research. The research shows that each learning situation has one "right" answer and, by applying it, each learner can achieve the same outcomes. To others, design is an art. Design choices are influenced by a variety of situational factors. They use intuition to guide design, and, because each learner and learning situation is different, expect that outcomes may vary among learners. Rowland (1993) observed that design is part science and part art.

Different instructional designers have different beliefs about how to best present content to learners. These beliefs range from a classical approach, like lecturing, to an individualistic approach, like experiential learning. These approaches can be considered on a continuum, which is presented in figure 2-1.

If in theory, design is part science and part art, and if it is guided by beliefs about how to best present content to learners, in practice, ISD is actually just problem solving (Rowland, 1993). That is, someone who needs training—the sponsor, who has authority to fund or stop funding on the project—presents you with a challenge and your job is to effectively and efficiently address that situation with a learning program.

Figure 2-1. A continuum of approaches to the ISD process.

Instructional Design Approaches

Technological Model	**Pragmatic Model**	**Individualist Model**
Focused on observable and measurable actions, and looks for a single "correct" solution to each problem	Integrates approaches of both ends of the spectrum: focused, when possible, on observable goals and data-driven decisions while remaining sufficiently flexible to address specific needs of the learner and learning context	Focused on meeting individual needs of learners; courses need to be tailored to unique needs of users

Like all good problem solving, the quality of the instructional design depends on the completeness of your definition of the problem and the closeness of the match between your solution and the issues identified in the definition. The ISD process provides a framework for defining the problem and preparing a solution.

WHY A DESIGN PROCESS IS IMPORTANT FOR E-LEARNING

Using a process to design e-learning is important. In a classroom, puzzled looks, shocked expressions, and drooping eyes all suggest that something about the course is missing the mark, and an astute instructor immediately changes course. But no such opportunity exists online; most of the content is "hard coded" and cannot be changed until a later version. Only by finding out about the learners and their needs first (including the technology available to them and their experience with it), developing content to meet those needs, testing the course before it is released, and verifying your assumptions with sponsors and potential learners at various checkpoints along the way can you minimize the risk of problems. To do so, course developers follow a process.

Similarly, the development of online courses requires the coordination of resources among training, information systems, and other groups within an organization. Only through a process can you make sure that the right people are available when you need them. In other words, a process is primarily a framework for coordinating resources and uncovering creative ideas at those times when they can be most easily incorporated into a project.

FOUR PHASES OF ISD FOR E-LEARNING

The process for designing e-learning is generally the same as that for classroom courses. The primary differences pertain to the types of issues you consider at each phase and the types of production (preparation for publication) and testing needed as you ready the online learning program for use. The process is divided into these four categories of activities:

1. *Definition phase:* Analyze and define the learning problem as concretely as possible, identify issues that will affect the project, and set goals to fill performance gaps.
2. *Design phase:* Devise a solution, gain approval from sponsors, and codify key design decisions to enable others to follow a consistent approach.
3. *Development phase:* Develop an e-learning program that conforms to the plans established in the design phase. Solicit feedback on the program and revise it as needed.
4. *Implementation and maintenance phase:* Duplicate the learning program, distribute it to learners, track its use, and revise the content as the needs of the organization dictate.

The next several sections present each of the phases. Figure 2-2 provides a visual representation of the ISD process for e-learning.

The Definition Phase

E-learning, just like traditional training, begins with a definition phase to identify needs, set goals, and prepare initial evaluation instruments, such as test questions. But, some of the issues you must analyze for e-learning pertain to technology available for designing and delivering instruction, the conduciveness of the learning environment to self-study, and the attitudes toward e-learning. The final step of the definition phase is preparation of a needs analysis report.

Conducting a Needs Analysis. This activity initiates the design and development process. When completed, you should have identified the following information:

- *Sponsor's business goal:* How will the e-learning program affect the bottom line of the sponsor? It affects the bottom line in one (and only one) of these ways: generating revenue (such as sales training), containing expenses (such as procedures and technical training), or complying with regulations (such as safety training). This is the ultimate need driving the sponsor's request for an e-learning program and, as suggested by performance consultants Robinson and Robinson, your online learning program must directly link to it (1989). Because up-front costs for e-learning efforts are often substantially higher than for classroom courses, aligning a proposed project with business needs becomes especially important, so sponsors can see clearly the business benefit and feel more comfortable funding a proposed e-learning project.
- *Performance gap:* The difference between the desired and current performance is called the *performance gap* (Dick & Carey, 1990). Any proposed e-learning solution should attempt to close this gap.

Figure 2-2. An overview of the ISD process for e-learning.

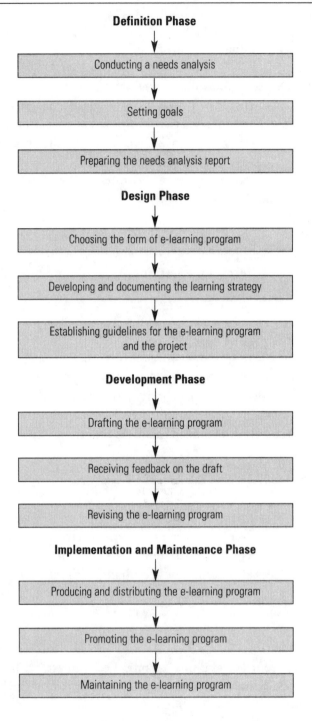

■ *Task analysis:* This analysis enumerates tasks that learners must perform to achieve the desired performance. In some instances, when the tasks involve physical actions, the list of tasks is clear. In other instances, when the tasks are intellectual ones, such as choosing the right model of computer to meet a customer's needs, task analysis is more of a challenge. A complete task analysis begins with a description of the situation that drives learners into the online learning program, then presents a hierarchy of tasks, including the primary task (that is, the overall task of the course), main tasks (ones that learners must complete to achieve the primary task), and supporting tasks (tasks that learners must complete to successfully complete the main tasks).

■ *Learners and the influences on them:* This information identifies to whom the content is directed and what would cause these people to accept or reject the content. At the least, you need to compile demographic information about the learners, including their proficiency with technology. At the most, you should develop character sketches (profiles) of learners so you can develop mental pictures of them, too (Cooper, 1999).

■ *Learning environment:* The area in which learners will most likely use the online learning program, such as a workplace or a learning center, must figure into your analysis of needs.

■ *Constraints on the project:* Identify the editorial, technical, and business issues affecting the project, such as corporate intranet guidelines that the learning project must follow, technology infrastructure, not-to-exceed budget, drop-dead completion date, and the corporate culture.

Setting Goals. With a sound understanding of the situation you need to address, you can set concrete goals for the project. Setting the goals has two main components: defining objectives and developing a plan for evaluating the results.

When you define objectives, define both the business objective and content objectives. The business objective is the business goal identified earlier, stated with more precision. The content objectives are the tasks you identified earlier, stated with more precision so that you can measure whether learners can successfully perform them.

Before you make any decisions about the structure of the content and the way you plan to present it, design the tools for assessing whether the learning program is effective. Training organizations evaluate their courses in a variety of ways but most use Kirkpatrick's (1998) familiar four levels of evaluation: reaction, learning, behavior, and results.

Defining objectives and planning evaluations are generally the same for online learning programs as for classroom courses, but the methods for collecting evaluation data differ.

Preparing the Needs Assessment Report. Once your analyses are complete and the goals are set, prepare a report to summarize the findings of the definition phase and to state the observable and measurable goals. The report should include drafts of the assessment tools you have developed.

This report identifies for the sponsor the assumptions and constraints under which you plan to operate as you design the learning program. Because incorrect assumptions lead to off-track designs, verifying those assumptions with your sponsor now can reduce rework and possible fractured work relations as you proceed with the project.

Deliverables of the Definition Phase. The primary deliverable for this phase of the process is a report of the needs analysis describing findings of the needs analysis and stating the observable and measurable goals developed.

This report identifies for the sponsor the assumptions and constraints under which you plan to operate when you design the e-learning program. Because incorrect assumptions lead to off-track designs, verifying those assumptions with your sponsor now can reduce rework and possible fractured work relations as you proceed with the e-learning project.

The Design Phase

During the design phase, you develop a blueprint for the learning program. Like its counterpart in building design, a blueprint for a learning program presents the plans for its structure, shows how the program will look, and identifies the standards to which it must be developed. Blueprints are especially important to online learning programs, because media-rich, asynchronous learning programs are complex and can take up to 11 times longer to develop than classroom courses. Key provisions of the learning plan include choosing the form of the e-learning program, the learning strategy, and the guidelines under which you will develop the e-learning program. (Note that this description of the design process assumes that you are developing an asynchronous course.)

Choosing the Form of the E-Learning Program. During this activity, you determine the form that the learning program should take. You should take into account such issues as:

- What type of e-learning program do you plan to develop—a self-guided tutorial, a chat-based tutorial, or, perhaps, a series of quick references? This choice matters because learners bring certain expectations to a particular form of learning program. For example, during a live course, learners expect to be actively engaged in a conversation. During this phase, you explicitly state the type of form you have chosen and the expectations that learners bring to it to increase the likelihood that your designs will meet learners' expectations.
- Verify that you are using the correct medium for communication even if the original request was for an online course. In some cases, despite the request, online learning might not be the most appropriate option for your sponsor. In addition to verifying the medium for the request, you also can identify

some issues arising from this choice. Also take a few moments to consider the positive and negative characteristics of the online reading experience to make sure that your designs emphasize the positive and address the negative.

Developing and Documenting the Learning Strategy. During this phase, you finally design the learning program. For some, this is the most creative phase because you determine how the e-learning program will look and how content will be presented. The learning strategy should include the following:

- *An outline or information map:* This is a diagram of the way content flows, including the introductory and summary screens.
- *A sample section:* Prepare a topic or lesson as if it were ready to be published. The sample section serves as a model for the finished learning program. In some cases, you might prepare a few versions of the sample section to show alternative treatments of the same content. Usually, you show the sample section to the sponsor for approval and to prospective learners to determine whether it will accomplish the intended goals.
- *Storyboards:* These aids help you plan for each additional screen in the learning program that is not included in the sample section. Each storyboard identifies the objectives to be addressed, how the content will be presented, audio and visual materials used on that screen (if any), and programming instructions (such as links to Web addresses). If you decide to use a course that has already been developed, you would not need to develop storyboards unless you plan to create a customized version of the course.

Note that sample sections and storyboards provide much more detail than might be provided during the design of a classroom course. However, this additional detail proves to be an effective planning tool and helps you to ensure the strategy will succeed with learners.

Establishing Guidelines for the E-Learning Project. After you receive the sponsor's approval on the design plans, you can complete the blueprint for your learning program. The last part of the blueprint includes guidelines for the project: ones that address editorial consistency and error-free operation of the e-learning program. These guidelines include the following:

- *Style guide:* This reference describes how recurring editorial issues are addressed in a given learning program (or in a series of related learning programs). These issues might include terminology, punctuation, capitalization, bibliographic references, use of numbers, and formatting of headings and text.
- *Templates:* Templates translate style guidelines into fill-in-the-blank forms, of sorts, for course developers. Templates simplify development and ensure that similar material is presented in consistent ways. Standard information is

already included on the screen, so course developers add only the information that's different.

- *Authoring platform specifications:* Adhering to specifications ensures that course developers working in different locations can easily exchange information or a platform can be easily created again if necessary. These specifications include the type of computer on which the content is developed and the software used to create it.
- *Viewing platform:* This set of specifications describes the type of software and hardware that learners need to view the course.
- *Printing specifications:* This set of specifications addresses any printed materials that accompany the course.

You would consider some of these guidelines when developing a classroom course, such as a style guide that addresses common terminology issues. Other guidelines are unique to online learning programs, like specifications for the authoring and viewing platforms.

Identifying members of the project team and establishing project guidelines for the budget and schedule at this point in the process significantly increases the accuracy of these projections. If you were to estimate these costs earlier, you would not have such accurate information, and estimates could be off by as much as 20 to 25 percent (Foshay, 1997).

Deliverables of the Design Phase. The deliverable of the design phase is a blueprint for a learning program. The blueprint consists of the following items:

- explicit statement of the form and the expectations learners bring
- description of the form and the expectations people bring to it.
- outline or information map
- sample section
- storyboards
- style guide
- specifications
- schedule
- budget
- list of project team members.

This blueprint becomes a contract for the project. All development efforts must conform to the blueprint. Similarly, this blueprint gives you leverage to change the scope of the project should you receive requests by the sponsor for additional material or a change to the blueprint.

At this time, you should also begin distributing regular reports on the status of the project to stakeholders to keep them informed about the progress of the project and to help them feel actively involved in it.

The Development Phase

Drafting the E-Learning Program. During this activity, you turn the plans for a learning program into a complete draft. Among the issues that you need to consider when you prepare the draft are

- *Reading and viewing online:* Online reading and viewing patterns differ from classroom learning. You need to adjust your communication style to the characteristics of the medium.
- *Clarity in communication:* Learners in asynchronous courses have no direct access to you or your verbal cues. Your communication style online must be less ambiguous than for more traditional learning situations.
- *Production of draft visual components:* You should wait to produce the most labor-intensive audio and visual materials until later in the process to ensure they will be produced without errors on the first try.
- *Programming for test questions and links:* You can now begin programming test questions and checking links identified during the design phases with a high level of confidence that no change will occur.

Receiving Feedback on the Draft. During this activity, you seek feedback on the draft of the learning program and respond to that feedback. Specifically, you should arrange for the following:

- technical reviews by subject matter experts (SMEs) who examine the draft learning program to assess the accuracy of the content
- editorial review, which identifies inaccuracies and inconsistencies in grammar and style of the text and visuals
- technical testing, which determines whether the learning software actually works
- usability testing, which tracks the speed and accuracy achieved by representative learners as they are observed going through the learning program, assesses their reactions to the learning program.

Revising the E-Learning Program. During this activity, you manage technical and editorial changes so you can balance the need to present information effectively and accurately with the need to limit the amount of rework and produce a learning program on time and within budget. Any necessary access aids, such as indexes and tables of contents, should also be prepared at this time. The revision process also includes development of course elements, or "boilerplate" sections, which are not directly related to the course content. Such items as the copyright notice, course description, and title screen fall into this category. It is also possible that you may have to undertake two or more revisions, requiring additional reviews of the draft learning program.

Deliverables of the Development Phase. The result of this phase is a completed and approved text; simple visuals; and approval to prepare complex and costly photographs, narration, and video sequences.

The Implementation and Maintenance Phase

Producing and Distributing the E-Learning Program. During this activity, you begin with a draft and conclude with the golden code, the materials that are ready to be distributed to learners. Specifically, this phase involves preparing the text, graphics, programming, and audiovisual components of the learning program for publication. After they are tested, these components are assembled into a master copy (if the components were not brought together during the draft process, as in the case for courses that include staged video) in a form that can be published on the Web or duplicated on CD or DVD.

The extent to which you participate in these activities depends on the way your sponsors structure these tasks. You may only provide a draft copy with instructions to a production specialist or you may produce the final draft and publish it yourself. Whatever the extent of your involvement, the better you understand this activity, the more effectively you can produce information. Also during this activity, you first duplicate the master copy of the learning program. This task may involve posting the learning programs on an intranet, extranet, or Internet site; or "burning" a CD-ROM or DVD with the learning materials. Any related print materials, such as CD jackets or accompanying workbooks, are also duplicated at this time.

Promoting the E-Learning Program. During this activity, you make learners aware of a learning program. You also follow up to see if the intended users are using and applying the e-learning program successfully. Specifically, this phase involves

- conducting a "postmortem," or a special meeting of the people who developed the course to determine what worked and what you would handle differently on future projects
- tracking response by learners to the e-learning program
- monitoring the need for technical changes in future editions of the e-learning program
- planning revisions to the learning program and scheduling their debuts.

Promoting an online learning program is similar to promoting a classroom course, but the follow-up becomes especially important because you do not have the classroom situation in which to request feedback and debrief learners.

Maintaining the E-Learning Program. After a course is published, you might need to make changes. In some cases, learners encounter errors that affect the learning experience. In other cases, the technical content changes. These activities occur in classroom courses, too, but the deadline of an upcoming class ensures that the changes are eventually made. Unless maintenance is scheduled for e-learning courses, developers who have moved onto new assignments might indefinitely postpone making these changes.

ACHIEVING EFFICIENCIES IN THE ISD PROCESS

Admittedly, designing e-learning requires extensive effort from all the project team members counter to what some software developers' promotional materials seem to indicate. Vendors of software for course development, as well as others in the industry, are fond of saying that e-learning simplifies design and development of courses. What they don't say is that efficiencies are not realized unless you design an e-learning course as part of a larger curriculum, and after you have developed several courses.

When you design courses as part of a larger effort, you can make use of existing designs and significantly reduce the time needed to develop a course. For example, you can reuse some of the results of the needs assessment conducted during the definition phase. You may be able to reuse some of the information collected during the design phase about the type of product and medium to be used for the e-learning project. You may be able to adapt an existing information map and reuse the sample section. Additionally, the guidelines developed during the design phase may apply to future e-learning projects because you have tested the designs and are assured of their effectiveness. But, these efficiencies experienced in later development efforts require a more involved design effort on earlier online programs.

THE LIMITATIONS OF A PROCESS

A process is a model of the real world. Models provide a framework for approaching situations and a list of issues to consider. With a model as a basis for planning your work, you significantly increase the likelihood of success on a project because you will perform the appropriate tasks at the appropriate times. The process also ensures that you verify assumptions about the content, learners, and project at appropriate times, before you have invested yourself intellectually, financially, and emotionally in a project.

But, as Gustafson (1991) notes, models of the ISD process are only representations of the real world. Although this process reflects what happens during the design and development of e-learning programs, it prescribes, to some extent, how those activities should occur. Your experience as you go through this process may differ according to your needs and those of your sponsors. The information you need to do your job might not be available at the appropriate times in the process and, as a result, you may have to alter the project timeline. The purpose of presenting a process is not to constrain you, but to help structure your work.

Similarly, you may find that you need to perform additional steps not listed in this process. The process is not intended to address every situation that might arise in your project; rather, it is intended to develop your understanding of the issues involved in designing and developing learning programs. When situations arise that are not addressed by this model, the process provides you with enough familiarity of the issues to make a good judgment about how to proceed.

YOUR TURN

This chapter presented the key phases and activities for the ISD process: definition (analyzing organizational needs and setting goals), design (choosing the type of learning, developing and documenting the learning strategy, and developing guidelines), development (drafting the learning program, receiving feedback, and revising the learning program), and implementation and maintenance (duplicating and distributing e-learning, and promoting and maintaining the online learning program).

Designing for e-learning using a process means that you ask the right questions at the right time to verify assumptions. Furthermore, it prompts you to get key stakeholder buy-in before proceeding with any design.

Now use worksheet 2-1 to think through the four phases of ISD and how they might apply to an e-learning project you have in mind. Consider sponsors' goals; possible organizational needs; your organization's culture; and potential constraints in terms of budget, schedule, and staffing. This run-though should be conceptual only at this point because you will get a chance to develop more detailed plans in later chapters. When you are finished, you should see that you are already on your way to successfully designing e-learning.

Worksheet 2-1. Applying the e-learning ISD process in your organization.

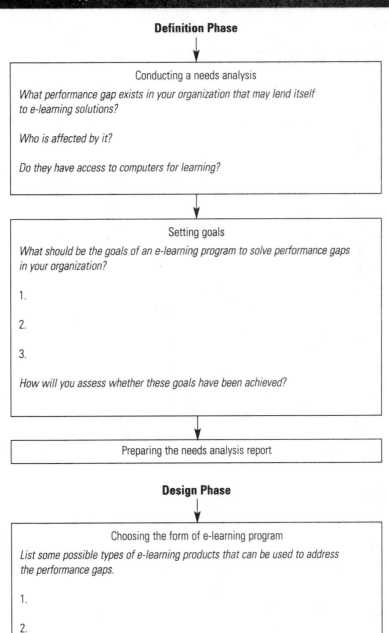

Definition Phase

Conducting a needs analysis

What performance gap exists in your organization that may lend itself to e-learning solutions?

Who is affected by it?

Do they have access to computers for learning?

Setting goals

What should be the goals of an e-learning program to solve performance gaps in your organization?

1.

2.

3.

How will you assess whether these goals have been achieved?

Preparing the needs analysis report

Design Phase

Choosing the form of e-learning program

List some possible types of e-learning products that can be used to address the performance gaps.

1.

2.

3.

(continued on next page)

Worksheet 2-1. Applying the e-learning ISD process in your organization (continued).

Developing and documenting the learning strategy

What resources can you tap as you develop and document your e-learning strategy?

1.

2.

3.

Establishing guidelines for the e-learning program and the project

Consider some guidelines and specifications that will ensure editorial consistency and error-free operation of the e-learning program:

1.

2.

3.

Development Phase

Drafting the e-learning program

How will you adapt your teaching style or writing style for the computer?

1.

2.

3.

Receiving feedback on the draft

What sources of feedback will be most relevant for evaluating your e-learning program?

1.

2.

3.

Revising the e-learning program

Implementation and Maintenance Phase

Producing and distributing the e-learning program

How will you distribute the materials—through the Web or by CD or DVD?

1.

2.

3.

Promoting the e-learning program

How can you let learners know that your program is available?

1.

2.

3.

Maintaining the e-learning program

What information do you anticipate will change after the course is published? When?
How much effort will be required to update the course?

1.

2.

3.

3

Conducting a Needs Analysis: Asking the Right Questions

Designing e-learning programs is complex, even for a first project. Because learners often take them without the benefit of a live instructor, e-learning programs must be significantly clearer than classroom courses to avoid misunderstandings and errors in learning. Learning content can also be tailored to address different applications, individual learning styles, and varying needs. Because technology affects both the development and delivery of learning material, technology requirements must be identified before any design and development can begin. And, because online learning programs typically require larger development budgets than classroom courses, missteps in design and development early on have costly implications later.

The more information you learn early, the better you can address these and other issues affecting the online learning program. The process of collecting this information is called *needs analysis.* Only by learning as much as possible about the project and then defining it in observable, measurable terms before proceeding to the design phase can you ensure that the online learning program will improve workplace performance as the sponsor has requested. The next several sections introduce you to the seven issues into which you must inquire as part of a needs analysis:

1. Clarify the request.
2. Identify the business need.
3. Identify the performance gap.
4. Conduct a task analysis.
5. Describe the learners.
6. Describe the learning environment.
7. Identify project constraints.

Check the book's companion Website (http://saulcarliner.home.att.net/oll/index .html) to view an example of a completed needs analysis. Specifically, the example shows how an instructional designer described each of the seven issues.

The next chapter explains how to turn the information you learned in analyzing the needs into a set of requirements for the proposed online learning program.

ISSUE 1: CLARIFY THE REQUEST

The first step in analyzing the needs underlying a request to develop an online learning program is restating the request. When doing so, use the exact words that the sponsor has used.

For example, if a sponsor has asked you to develop a "two-part sales training course, one of which focuses on the product and another that focuses on techniques for relationship marketing," you would begin this part by stating that you have been asked to develop a "two-part sales training course, one of which focuses on the product and another that focuses on techniques for relationship marketing." At this point, you can expand on the request.

Using the same words that the sponsor used is a way of saying, "I listened to your request and understand what you have said." Few things build confidence and trust the way that type of listening does. However, repeating the request using the sponsor's words does not mean that the final project must take the form of the action requested. For example, a sponsor might request that you design and develop a synchronous course but you believe that the sponsor's needs would be met by an asynchronous one. Using the sponsor's words now offers an opportunity to later persuade the sponsor that an alternative might better fit the sponsor's needs. The sponsor is more likely to take your suggestions later if the sponsor now believes that you understand the initial request.

In addition, as you restate the request, you should also clarify it to make sure that you fully understand it. If there's a question about the specific request or the intended learners, clarify it now. Although later areas of inquiry will also explore these issues, by clarifying now you make sure that you're asking questions about the right issues.

ISSUE 2: IDENTIFY THE BUSINESS NEED

An e-learning course is more likely to be effective from a business standpoint if it addresses a revenue or cost problem that the business currently faces. The best time to establish this link is at the very beginning of an effort to develop an online learning program—before you even consider the content. The stronger the link between the program and business needs, the stronger the support for the project is likely to be. The project should be tied to one of three categories of business goals (table 3-1).

When identifying a business need, choose one of the three—and only one. Many sponsors would like a single course to address several business needs, but if you try to do too much, the risk of failure increases.

Also, when identifying the business need, try to state the desired result in tangible, measurable terms. Here's an example of a business need for a project: "The new

Table 3-1. Types of business goals.

Generating Revenue	Some course development efforts are intended to increase revenue to the organization. For example, sales representatives usually participate in product training courses to help them sell those products.
Containing Expenses	Some course development efforts are intended to increase staff productivity, reduce the number of errors, or increase self-sufficiency without relying on costly, in-person help. For example, user training for software is intended to reduce reliance on the more costly support services, such as the help line.
Complying with Regulations	Some course development efforts are required by government, industry, or corporate guidelines. For example, occupational safety and health courses are often mandated by law; and mandated "right-to-know" courses inform workers of dangerous chemicals in their workplaces and how to safely work with them.

employee orientation for our organization is intended to contain expenses by ensuring more consistent performance among new workers and by reducing the labor needed to train them." The more tangible the result, the more likely that the business will see the benefit of the completed course.

The business need also suggests the general budget for the project. If the goal is to generate revenue, the project budget will probably be high. If the goal is to contain expenses, the budget likely will be in the moderate range; and the goal of complying with regulations usually involves a low budget.

In many instances, a sponsor will not be concerned with a business need. Identify it anyway. At some later time in the project, the sponsor may have difficulty understanding the business need for the project. This is especially true for e-learning projects, which typically necessitate larger up-front investments than classroom courses. By establishing a business need at the beginning of a project, that concern is less likely to emerge.

The business need should not be confused with the business case. The business case is an economic justification for producing the course. The business goal is just one part of the business case. The business case must take into account the costs associated with the e-learning project, including those listed in table 3-2. It is usually prepared after the needs analysis is complete.

ISSUE 3: IDENTIFY THE PERFORMANCE GAP

The performance gap is the gap between current and ideal performance (Dick & Carey, 1990). The training that the sponsor requested ultimately must bridge that gap. For this reason, as you start to consider the content and users, one of the first things you need to consider is what good performance looks like and what performance looks like now.

Labor Costs	**Production and Distribution Costs**	**Delivery Costs**	**Other Development Costs**
• Instructional designer time • Course developer time • Project management time • Editorial services • Graphic design services • Production costs	• Copying charges • Distribution of review materials • Packaging costs • Printing costs • Inventory costs • Internal or external marketing	• Learning time for learner • Travel time to learning center • Maintenance and overhead for building (if any)	• Usability testing • Equipment and software purchases • Training costs

Table 3-2. Cost elements to consider in the business case for e-learning programs.

One way to think of this is like taking two snapshots, one "before" and one "after." The "before" picture describes the current results and the process by which performers reach them. The snapshot also describes the environment in which people work and imparts some information about their motivation to perform well (or lack of motivation). This information might become relevant later as you come to understand why people are not performing in the ideal way. If you have several groups of learners performing the task in different ways, you might take several before pictures.

The "after" picture describes the performance desired by the sponsor. It should first describe the results that people achieve in an ideal environment. Then, it briefly describes the process by which performers reach those results. (In the next area of inquiry, you'll explore this process in more detail.) Last, this snapshot describes the ideal environment in which people work. This information might become relevant later; some aspects of this work environment can affect the choice of teaching strategy.

As for each issue in the needs analysis, visit the companion Website (http://saulcarliner.home.att.net/oll/index.html) for a sample needs analysis, including a description of a performance gap.

ISSUE 4: CONDUCT A TASK ANALYSIS

In this area of inquiry, you identify the specific tasks (or processes) that learners must follow to achieve ideal performance. Specifically, you work with expert performers and SMEs to identify the sequence of the tasks that learners go through to achieve ideal performance. You might observe them, interview them, and try the tasks yourself to develop an ideal process. In some cases, you might need to fill in gaps in the content that other sources do not address.

To make sure that you have the appropriate broad perspective, the first task you identify is the primary task. The primary task is the key thing that learners must be able to perform after completing the online learning program. For example, the primary task for word-processing training is preparing documents. The primary task for new manager training is leading a department.

Next, you identify the main tasks, the processes that learners must perform to successfully achieve the primary task. Generally, a primary task consists of five to nine main tasks. For example, the main tasks for word processing might be creating new documents, changing documents, checking spelling, formatting documents, printing documents, and saving documents. The main tasks for new managers might be preparing work plans, assigning and tracking work, performing supervisory tasks, budgeting, and reporting department progress.

Then, you identify supporting tasks. Supporting tasks are processes that learners must perform to successfully master a given main task. Generally, a main task has between five and nine supporting tasks. For example, the supporting tasks for formatting a document might include checking margins, choosing type fonts, preparing paragraphs, preparing lists and tables, indicating headings, and adding page numbers. Because some supporting tasks are more complex than can be adequately conveyed in a single task, you can further divide supporting tasks into sub- and sub-sub supporting tasks.

The tasks come in three categories:

> ## Six Methods of Uncovering Performance Gaps
>
> - *Interviews:* Conduct formal interviews with as many people who have information to share as possible. Typically, these people would be the sponsor, SMEs, and prospective learners.
> - *Focus groups:* Focus groups are a special type of interview in which you interview as a group eight people who are demographically similar. A focus group usually lasts two hours and can cover three to five questions.
> - *Surveys:* A survey involves asking a select group of people to respond to a series of questions that can be easily scored. The responses are recorded and analyzed.
> - *A day in the life:* One of the ways to learn about a subject's work is to experience it. A technique that comes from the usability community, it involves following someone through his or her daily routine from the start of the work day until the end of it (Wilson, 2001).
> - *Internship:* Sometimes only an extended immersion in the environment provides sufficient background for preparing a learning program. The person taking the internship usually has specific responsibilities to make the experience more meaningful.
> - *Artifact analysis:* This term from anthropological research merely means reviewing reports, memos, screenshots from computer programs, examples of other training, and other evidence that can provide useful insights into the content or the learners.

- *Physical:* Also called psychomotor tasks, these tasks are performed by hand or some other physical activity.
- *Intellectual or cognitive:* Such tasks are performed mentally, such as choosing the right model of computer to meet a customer's needs or matching symptoms with a diagnosis.
- *Attitudinal or affective:* These tasks are about the learner's attitude. Usually, affective tasks are redefined as cognitive or psychomotor tasks.

The result is a hierarchy of tasks, starting with the primary tasks at the top of the list and working down to sub-sub supporting tasks. In addition to identifying these tasks, you also need to do the following:

- Identify tasks that learners are assumed to already be able to perform. These are called entry tasks, and you can list these as assumed or prerequisite knowledge.
- If several paths to successful performance exist, choose one and only one to address as the preferred method. For example, one can cut and paste in a word processor by choosing menu items, using icons on the button bar, or using keyboard controls. All three are correct, but confronting learners with all three at once will likely confuse them. Choose the one preferred method—most likely, the easiest.

Although the task analysis is a standard part of most instructional design efforts, it plays a crucial role in the design of effective e-learning. Because learners may not have direct interaction with instructors as they go through an online learning program, it must be especially clear. Missing information in the task analysis now usually results in incomplete content later. A sample task analysis is available on the accompanying Website.

ISSUE 5: DESCRIBE THE LEARNERS

In addition to learning about the content, you need to learn about the learners. Specifically, you need to collect demographic data about the learners, and prepare prose descriptions of them.

Reporting Demographics

When describing learners, instructional designers typically characterize them with demographic data, such as job title, length of experience, assumed knowledge, gender (if relevant), language skills (if relevant), and cultural affiliations (if appropriate). In some cases, your learning program has one group of learners. In such situations, you prepare a single set of demographics. In other cases, your learning program has several groups of learners. In such situations, you prepare a set of demographics for each primary group of learners.

As part of your demographic description of learners, also consider the learners' relationship to the content and interest in it. Table 3-3 will help you identify learners' relationship to the content.

Later, when you develop the learning product, you should match the level and tone of the content to the users' relationship to it. For example, most end users of corporate applications are decision receivers. They did not choose the software they use nor did they participate in the decision to purchase it. This lack of involvement needs

Table 3-3. The relationship between learners and the use of course content.

Decision Maker	Someone who will use the content to make decisions for others
Decision Influencer	Someone who will use the content to offer meaningful suggestions to others who in turn can use the information to make decisions
Decision receiver	Someone who is using the content because he or she has been told he or she must

to be addressed. Similarly, a course on business cases is intended for decision influencers—people who prepare recommendations for decision makers. The course needs to acknowledge the importance of using the business case to persuade a decision maker to a particular point of view.

Also consider learners' appetite for the content. Unlike classroom learners who usually receive time off work to take a course, online learners must fit learning activities into their everyday routine. They have little patience for learning products that present inappropriate information or information at an inappropriate level of detail. For informal (optional) learning, learners simply drop out. By matching the level of content with learners' appetite for it, they are more likely to finish. Specifically, learners have three levels of appetite for content as shown in table 3-4 (Wilson, 1994).

Later, when you develop the course, you should match the quantity of content to the learners' appetite for it. For example, a course on computer systems for end users

Table 3-4. Learners' appetites for content.

Nibbler	Someone who wants to learn the least amount necessary to achieve the desired performance and focuses on *how* rather than *why* (unless absolutely necessary). An example of a nibbler is a customer service representative learning about the procedure for handling an incoming call. The majority of learners in a training context are nibblers.
Grazer	Someone who wants to get a high-level picture of a topic area but who will not directly use the content. An example of a grazer is a manager who needs familiarity with the key areas of artificial intelligence, but who will not be writing programs using it. Grazers are the second largest audiences for training.
Hungry Heifer	Someone who wants to know everything about a subject, either because the learner is going to have to answer the most difficult questions about the subject or because the learner wants to appear on the television show "Jeopardy." Hungry heifers constitute a small number in the training audience.

may provide a nibbler's quantity of content—just enough to use the system. A course for managers might emphasize concepts and uses of the software but may not include operating instructions if the manager is not going to use the software. And, a course for technical support staff needs to provide extensive detail because they will have to answer questions that are not be covered in the documentation.

Influences Affecting Learners

Some influences on learners come from the business. An example is a recent reorganization that results in new work for a group. Some of these influences are cultural. For example, when two companies merge, they usually have different cultures that play a role in acceptance of the content in learning programs. To be successful, you need to address these influences when you design the program.

E-learning designers need to be especially sensitive to these issues, because the computer presents content anonymously, and when learners have a negative reaction to it they tend to react more strongly than they might in person (Sproull & Kiesler, 1992). Furthermore, because no instructor is present when learners read such content, you have no means of immediately responding to the unanticipated negative reactions that an online learning program may spark.

Character Sketches of Learners

One way to get to know learners in greater depth than is possible through a list of demographics is to create character sketches. You create character sketches of three learners in each primary audience: a low-maintenance learner (one who needs little attention), an average learner, and a high-maintenance learner (one who needs a great deal of attention) (Cooper, 1999).

If a proposed online learning program has several primary groups of learners, prepare separate character sketches for each primary group, just as you would prepare a separate set of demographics. By separating this information now, you can later see whether content for one group will be appropriate for the other or whether the content needs to be adjusted. One of the strengths of e-learning is its ability to personalize content, but personalization is only effective if course developers really understand the intended learners—what they have in common and what makes them unique.

As for each issue in the needs analysis, visit the companion Website (http://saulcarliner.home.att.net/oll/index.html) to view a sample needs analysis, including a description of the learners.

ISSUE 6: DESCRIBE THE LEARNING ENVIRONMENT

The environment in which people use the learning products also affects what you can design. Some environmental factors can limit your design. For example, if people work in a large "bullpen" environment, including audio clips in the learning product can be distracting to others in the work environment. Or, if a company has an intranet that everyone regularly checks, that intranet might be helpful in announcing and promoting the learning program. Specifically, you should look at the following types of issues in the learning environment:

- Where do you expect people to use the learning product: in their workplaces, at their homes, in a learning center, some other location, or wherever they choose?
- What distractions, such as ambient noise, interruptions, telephone calls, and so forth, exist in the work environment?
- Will the learner be alone in the environment or are others there? If others are in there, what are they doing? Could learning activities distract these other people?
- What types of technology already exist in the learning environment? Are any of these technologies available for learning? For example, most manufacturing floors have many computers on them, but they are exclusively used for manufacturing activities and their physical positions are not conducive to learning (they might positioned to be viewed while standing or in the middle of a larger monitoring station with several people working in close proximity).

ISSUE 7: IDENTIFY PROJECT CONSTRAINTS

In addition to identifying the performance gap, the tasks to be covered, and the learners, you also need to identify the constraints affecting the project. Specifically, you need to investigate these categories of constraints:

- editorial and graphics guidelines (style guidelines, corporate identity concerns, and prescribed screen designs)
- technology infrastructure (authoring software, database, programming language, plug-ins, hardware, and operating systems)
- business constraints (budget, deadlines, and available staffing)
- corporate culture.

Product Constraints

The first category of constraints is product constraints, which control what you can present and how you can present it. Editorial guidelines, called style guidelines, affect the usage of terminology, punctuation, and grammar. Sometimes these guidelines also set a standard structure for certain types of learning products, ensuring that similar learning products have a similar look.

The corporate communications departments in most medium and large corporations have established a style guide that describes the preferred ways of handling corporate terminology and similar matters. Most corporations also have a preferred dictionary and general style guide, from which they derived corporate guidelines. In most instances, online learning products must conform to these style guidelines.

Design guidelines affect the design of screens presented online. Most corporations want a family look to everything they publish, especially Websites that are produced by many different groups within the organization, but appear to users as if they are one. Specifically, corporate design guidelines specify which typefaces you should use and when; margins; use of colors, images, buttons and other standard elements on screens, and the corporate logo; and similar issues. In most organizations, the corporate communications department also maintains the corporate design guidelines.

Technology Infrastructure

The second category of constraints is the technology infrastructure in the organization. The technology infrastructure refers to the hardware and software that is standard in the organization. Whenever possible, organizations like to take advantage of this infrastructure and find a way to adapt it for online learning.

Specifically, you must consider the minimum configuration of learners' computers at the time you are scheduled to launch the learning product. That is, what hardware and software products are available to learners. If learners are internal, the IS group can provide this information. If the learners are external to your organization, marketing research can provide this information.

When considering the standard configuration, especially consider these issues related to the Internet:

- preferred browser (if any)
- bandwidth (telephone hookup, broadband access, or combination)
- standard plug-ins
- whether users' systems are compatible with video and audio files
- security on the network.

Also consider the authoring tools and other learning software that are already in use in the company. Some IS departments make purchases before the training department is ready to launch an e-learning effort.

Business Constraints

The third category of constraints is standard business constraints. These include

- the not-to-exceed budget (even if a sponsor claims to have none, press onward)
- the drop-dead deadline for completing the project
- staff who must participate in the design and development effort.

Corporate Culture

The last category of constraints encompasses items that you should not include in a report to sponsors. These are issues of corporate culture and the sponsor's history with previous projects that will affect your work. These issues include

- communication strategies within the organization
- attitude toward technology: technophilic (gung-ho on technology) or technophobic (Luddites)
- attitude toward technology-based learning like e-learning
- project history and tendency to make last-minute changes.

By identifying aspects of the corporate culture, you can assess the influence of your sponsor in the organization, the likelihood that technical information will change during the course of the project, and the behaviors you need to succeed in the organization (Hackos, 1994).

KEEP AN OPEN MIND

Although seven issues are provided in this chapter, this list only provides a starting point for your needs analysis. Because no two learning projects are alike, no single set of scripted questions can identify all of the needs underlying a project. Therefore, if you hear of something that you feel may be relevant as you go through this phase, explore it.

Similarly, keep an open mind as you go through the needs analysis. If you enter this phase with the solution already designed, then you will not ask the questions that might help you come up with the learning product best-matched to meet the needs, or you will tune out a valuable opportunity. Also, keep an open mind about the answers to the questions. Rather than entering this process for the purpose of confirming your answers, enter it to learn. You may find that your instincts are off.

YOUR TURN

This chapter described the seven key areas of questioning for a needs analysis and showed how they apply to an e-learning course. It also gave you some ways to reduce the risk that the project will not meet expectations.

To see examples of completed needs analyses, visit the companion Website at http://saulcarliner.home.att.net/oll/index.html.

Now it is your turn to think through your needs assessment at your organization. See if you can complete worksheet 3-1.

Worksheet 3-1. Applying the needs assessment process to your e-learning project.

Clarify the request.	Use the sponsor's words. _____ _____ _____
Identify the business need.	This project will provide the following benefit to the sponsor (check one and only one): ☐ Generate revenue ☐ Contain expenses ☐ Comply with regulations How? (Explain as tangibly as possible.) _____ _____
Identify the performance gap.	Current scenario: _____ _____ _____ Ideal scenario:_____ _____ _____
Conduct a task analysis.	Primary task : _____ Main task 1: _____ Supporting tasks: _____ _____ _____ _____ _____ _____ Main task 2: _____ Supporting tasks: _____ _____ _____ _____ _____ _____

Describe the learners.	Demographics: _____ Character sketches: (use additional paper if needed) _____ _____ _____ _____ _____
Describe the learning environment.	_____ _____ _____ _____ _____ _____
Identify project constraints.	Product constraints: ☐ Organizational editorial guidelines _____ ☐ Preferred style guide (such as the *Chicago Manual of Style* or the *MLA Style Guide*): _____ ☐ Preferred dictionary (such as the *American Heritage Dictionary* or *Merriam-Webster's Collegiate Dictionary*): _____ ☐ Organizational design guidelines (such as intranet or Internet guidelines): _____ Technical constraints: ☐ Authoring tools already in use in your organization (if any) : _____ _____ ☐ Learning management system in use (if any): _____ ☐ Configuration of learner's systems (especially the browsers available to learners (and their versions), plug-ins that learners can be assumed to have (such as Flash), and the availability of sound cards and other specialized hardware: _____ ☐ Network issues, such as a limit on the use of video or audio: _____ _____ Business constraints: ☐ Drop-dead end date: _____ ☐ Not-to-exceed budget:_____ ☐ Who must participate on the project: _____ _____ Corporate culture and project history: _____ _____

4

Setting Objectives and Preparing Evaluations

In the last chapter, you learned how to analyze the needs underlying the online learning program. Once that's complete, you're ready to begin designing the learning product. Right?

Not quite. Although you have determined what the learning product should accomplish, you need to formally state the goals for it. By establishing these goals, both the course development team and sponsor have a common agreement about the purpose of the learning product. Immediately after setting the goals—and before any design work begins—you also draft the evaluation instruments for the learning product. That is, you draft the satisfaction surveys, tests, and follow-up surveys. If the goals state what the learning product should do, the evaluations describe what successful achievement of those goals looks like (Mager, 1997a). With a concrete description of successful achievement, you can later design learning programs that are likely to result in this success.

Setting goals and drafting evaluations are the purposes of this second activity of the design and development phase. The first part of this chapter explains how to write objectives—the formal statements of goals; the second part explains how to draft evaluations.

How to Write Objectives

Objectives are the requirements that your online learning program must achieve. They represent a sort of guarantee to both your sponsor and learners. To your sponsors, objectives state what they can expect the learning program to accomplish. To learners, objectives state the new skills they can expect to develop after taking the course. As requirements, objectives represent the tangible outcomes of needs analysis and the focus of later design work. You can set two types of objectives for an online learning program: business, which state the intended business results; and content, which state the skills learners must master so that the business objectives are achieved.

Specifically, content objectives state the content that the proposed learning product must cover and the extent to which learners must master that material. Objectives for both e-learning and traditional training are written in a formal structured way, using language that reinforces observable and measurable outcomes. Each content objective follows a familiar three-part format:

1. Observable and measurable task
2. Conditions under which the task should be performed
3. Level of acceptable performance.

Here is an example: Install Word Plus (observable and measurable task) with the use of instructions (condition) within five minutes with no errors (level of acceptable performance).

The objectives are derived from tasks prepared as part of the needs analysis. In fact, the tasks themselves form the task of each objective. When preparing objectives, however, you also add the conditions and level of acceptable performance, giving you an opportunity to more thoroughly define the tasks.

For example, if the task was "Install a desktop computer," the objective might be "Using the documentation provided with it, install a desktop computer within 10 minutes without any errors."

Also, like the list of tasks developed earlier, the objectives form a hierarchy. Main tasks form the basis of *terminal objectives,* the key objectives that learners must master. Supporting tasks become *enabling objectives,* those that enable learners to complete the terminal objectives.

The practice of writing objectives was developed for formal learning, but it is easily adapted for informal learning. Objectives tell learners of the expectations that have been set for them. In a formal learning program, learners only succeed when they have mastered the objectives.

In informal learning, however, learners enter with their own goals. They set their own expectations so, in theory, objectives may not seem appropriate, at least on a philosophical level. However, writing objectives is still appropriate for informal learning materials. Although learners set their own goals, they can use the objectives to determine whether your objectives will meet their learning needs. Preparing objectives helps you, too, by identifying the content that needs to be covered.

If you are interested in digging deeper into writing objectives, see the companion Website for this book (http://saulcarliner.home.att.net/oll/index.html). Also see Robert Mager's (1997b) *Preparing Instructional Objectives: A Critical Tool in the Development of Effective Instruction.* You might also look into the constructivist approach to education, which advocates the use of outcomes, an alternative to formal objectives. Finally, see the sidebar, "Don't Forget to Set a Business Objective," for guidance on writing business objectives for an online learning program.

How to Prepare Evaluations

If learning objectives state the goals of the learning product, then evaluations establish what successful achievement of those objectives looks like. For example, if the objective of a course is "managing time so that no more than 20 percent of it is spent on priority *C* activities," success would entail managing a daily or weekly schedule that begins with deadlines but allows for interruptions by telephone calls, messages, co-workers, and household emergencies. The evaluation would ask learners how they would manage these interruptions.

In other words, evaluations present specific applications of the content. By designing evaluations in advance, course developers can "teach to the test"; that is, design courses so that learners are most likely to achieve the objectives. That's why instructional design models always suggest that instructional designers prepare evaluations before they begin designing a learning program. This section explains how to prepare evaluations for online learning programs. It first presents concepts underlying evaluations, then offers suggestions for evaluating online learning programs.

Concepts of Evaluation

Trainers evaluate their courses for a variety of reasons. First, they want to be sure that the learning product is effective, that it "worked." Specifically, they want to judge the learners' satisfaction with the program, the extent to which they mastered the learning content, how the learning program affected learners after they finished it, and whether the sponsoring organizations will realize a return on their

---

Don't Forget to Set a Business Objective

In addition to writing content objectives, course developers should develop a business objective that states in observable and measurable terms how the learning product will benefit the organization funding it. An online learning program may have many content objectives, but, as described in chapter 3, it should have a single business goal: to generate revenue, to contain expenses, or to comply with regulatory requirements.

The business objective states the business goal in observable and measurable terms, using the same three-part structure as content objectives. To help you focus on the business objective, you should write the business objective before you write the objectives for the content. By doing so, you will have better established the right focus for the content.

Consider some examples of business objectives:

- For generating revenue: Meet sales projections for the new product within six months.
- For containing expenses: Reduce the amount of rework by 30 percent within three months of administering the course.
- For complying with regulations: Achieve a 100 percent safety inspection in every department for the next 24 months.

Whenever possible, try to include financial figures in the business objectives. Because training is not an exact field and because many of your clients may not be aware of their full financial picture, you may not be able to propose specific financial or business targets for the online learning program. In such cases, describe how the organization benefits in less specific terms.

Be aware that some sponsors will not show much interest in your writing business objectives. Do it anyway; it is a subtle way of informing them that your ultimate goal is benefiting their business (Carliner, 1998).

investment in the learning program. For these reasons, evaluations must assess meaningful goals that the sponsors and course developers have agreed upon.

These issues certainly pertain to e-learning (Horton, 2001). Lacking the immediacy of classroom contact, developers of online learning programs need other sources of feedback about their work. Because many new online learning programs build from the designs of existing ones, designers need feedback about what works and what doesn't before proceeding with development. Finally, because of the large financial investments involved in online learning and the persistent skepticism about its effectiveness, evaluations provide insights into some of the long-term effects on learners and their impact on organizations.

One of the most popular frameworks for assessing learning is the classic four-level evaluation framework first proposed by Donald Kirkpatrick more than 40 years ago. The different types of evaluations in Kirkpatrick's (1998) model assess participants' reactions to the program, how much participants learned, how much of the learning they retain after a period of time, and the impact that the training program has on the bottom line of the organization. See table 4-1 for a quick review of Kirkpatrick's evaluation framework.

The Kirkpatrick model can be used to assess formal and informal learning, and it can be used assess e-learning. The following sections provide a quick review of how to draft evaluations for e-learning using the four levels of the Kirkpatrick model.

Level 1: Assessing Reaction

Almost every classroom course ends with a request that learners complete an evaluation, affectionately known as the "smiley face" survey. Actually, if done correctly, these surveys can explore participants' reactions to much more substantive issues including the following:

Table 4-1. Kirkpatrick's four levels of evaluation.

Level	Name	Issues Assessed at This Level
1	Reaction	Assesses participants' initial reactions to a course, also called a "smiley sheet"
2	Learning	Assesses the extent to which participants achieved the objectives
3	Transfer	Assesses the extent to which participants actually apply the lessons learned in a course
4	Business results	Assesses the financial impact of the training course on the bottom line of the organization

Source: Adapted from Kirkpatrick, D.L. (1998). Evaluating Training Programs: The Four Levels (2d edition). San Francisco: Berrett-Koehler.

- whether or not they learned anything
- the likelihood of applying the content
- effectiveness of particular instructional strategies
- effectiveness of the course "packaging."

Don't just ask for comments; pose more pointed questions. For example, ask what was most effective about the course and what one thing could be improved. By limiting the questions, participants generally offer detailed suggestions. If several participants comment on the same issue, it probably needs attention. Figure 4-1 contains a sample of a level 1 evaluation for an online learning product.

The most significant challenge in level 1 evaluation for e-learning is the response rate. Because classroom instructors control the exit to the classroom, participants feel compelled to respond, and response rates can approach as high as 100 percent. In the anonymous world of online learning, however, learners can easily ignore the feedback button or annoying attempts to require completion of an evaluation form before exiting the course.

What can work, instead, is this: For formal courses, electronically send an evaluation form to a statistically valid sample of all people who completed the learning program, and offer them an incentive for completing the evaluation form. Send follow-up reminders to ensure a high response rate. For informal courses, generally follow the same procedure, but choose the sample from people who started the learning product rather than those who completed it. In many informal learning situations, learners complete their own goals even though they do not complete yours.

Programs can be used to automatically identify the learners to be surveyed and generate the email and follow-up messages needed. Similarly, programs can automatically tally responses and provide reports suitable for distribution.

You might also explore other techniques of gauging learner satisfaction, such as focus groups and in-depth interviews.

Level 2: Assessing Learning

A substantive method of assessing whether participants learned the designated content is by evaluating their command of the content immediately after completing the learning program. Typically, this type of activity has been called testing, but because the term *testing* has such a negative connotation, try using the terms *evaluation* and *assessment*. The evaluation gauges whether someone learned something and, if the person needs additional work, identifies specific content on which to focus.

Assessing learning in meaningful ways poses a variety of challenges. What follows are just a few of these challenges:

- *Exactly when should the assessment be given?* Under ideal circumstances, participants take an assessment before beginning an assignment (called a *pretest*), but this is not always practical. Most trainers rely on tests administered after learners go through the content, called *posttesting*.

Figure 4-1. Sample of a level 1 evaluation for an e-learning product.

Your Opinions, Please

1. **In a word, how would you describe this course:** _____

2. **Using a number, how would you describe this course?**

1	2	3	4	5
Abysmal		Average		Outstanding

3. **How prepared for the certification exam did you feel *before* taking this course?**

1	2	3	4	5
Not at all		Somewhat prepared		Very prepared

4. **How prepared for the certification exam did you feel *after* taking this course?**

1	2	3	4	5
Not at all		Somewhat prepared		Very prepared

5. **How likely are you to use the information taught in this course on the job?**

1	2	3	4	5
Not at all		Not sure		Very likely

6. **Describe the experience of taking this course online:**

I have taken online courses before (circle one)   Yes   No

Rate the quality of the:

Content

1	2	3	4	5
Thrown together		OK		Superb

Lecture

1	2	3	4	5
Thrown together		OK		Superb

Video

1	2	3	4	5
Barely visible		OK		Crystal clear

Audio

1	2	3	4	5
Barely audible		OK		Crystal clear

Rate the usefulness of the:

Slides

1	2	3	4	5
Pure adornment		OK		Illustrative

Linked articles

	1	2	3	4	5
	Distracting		OK		Enlightening

Linked Websites

	1	2	3	4	5
	Distracting		OK		Enlightening

Rate the availability of the:

Course

	1	2	3	4	5
	Perpetually down		OK		Always available

Instructor (for the purpose of contacting by email)

	1	2	3	4	5
	Missing in action		There		Dependable

Overall, taking this course was:

Convenient

	1	2	3	4	5
	No way		Somewhat		Totally

Compared to a classroom course

	1	2	3	4	5
	Much worse		The same		Much better

I'd take another course online

	1	2	3	4	5
	I'd rather have surgery without anesthetic		If I must		In a heartbeat

7. **The best part of this course was:** _____

_____

_____

8. **This one thing that could improve this course most is:** _____

_____

_____

■ *What makes good test questions?* The only valid test questions emerge directly from the objectives. Because the objectives already suggest the test question, the questions are partially written. In practice, final assessments usually assess only the terminal objectives (main tasks). Because the enabling objectives (supporting tasks) are ones that enable a learner to complete a terminal objective; if learners demonstrate mastery of terminal objectives, they have essentially demonstrated mastery of the enabling objectives. (See the companion Website for examples showing how test questions can be derived from objectives.) In some cases, the questions look like traditional test questions, but for most e-learning, assessment of on-the-job performance is paramount. Scenarios in which learners must demonstrate their ability to perform the objectives within a real-world context make outstanding assessments of learning.

■ *How many test questions should be written?* To arrive at this answer, consider how many questions you may need for a given objective to ensure that the participants really learned the material. As part of this phase of the design process, you should develop several test questions to assess each objective. If you are going to randomly present questions to learners in a final exam, then you need to write at least three or four to provide a random question generator with several possible test questions. In addition, you might develop several additional questions that can be used for exercises.

■ *What kind of feedback should be provided?* In an assessment that will be used to determine whether a learner passes a formal course, instructors generally hold all feedback until the end so that knowledge of their early performance does not interfere with later questions. In an assessment primarily intended to help the learner assess his or her own learning, instructors generally provide feedback during the learning activity.

■ *How much feedback is enough?* The extent of the feedback varies, depending on the nature of the assessment and the independence of the learners. For example, learners in the middle of a computer simulation only need feedback if they have entered information incorrectly and the simulation cannot continue. In contrast, learners in a course on time management may value feedback throughout the assessment. When learners incorrectly answer questions, they may benefit from review. This review is called *remediation.*

E-learning offers a prime opportunity to take advantage of technology for carrying out level 2 evaluation. You can build evaluation measures right into the learning product by using authoring tools specifically designed for online learning. These tools have templates for asking nearly every type of objective question (that is, true/false, multiple choice, matching, or fill-in-the-blank) and providing users with feedback. Try using software that tracks users' keystrokes on Websites, and investigate learning management software that lets you track learners' scores and document successful completion for those who achieve a passing score.

Other specialized software lets you randomly generate test questions. Different learners see different questions for the same terminal objectives and, because no two learners get the same test, you are protected to some extent against cheating. Learning management software can provide targeted feedback to learners, and send them back to parts of the online learning program that teach the material that they answered incorrectly on the test. Other software even lets you automatically score essay tests and check for plagiarism in papers submitted by learners.

Level 3: Assessing Transfer to the Job

The ultimate value of training is the application of its lessons to the job. In some ways, a level 3 evaluation is similar to a level 2 evaluation in that it substantively assesses the learner's grasp of the content. The primary difference is that level 3 evaluation is performed several weeks or months after the level 2 evaluation. The amount of time separating the level 2 and level 3 evaluations can be set at the discretion of the course developer, though the earliest that a level 3 evaluation should be conducted is six weeks after training and the latest is six months.

A variety of techniques are used perform a level 3 evaluation. Two of the most common are

- observation of the performance of tasks covered by the course objectives
- surveys of learners, their supervisors, and co-workers, asking each of them how well the learner applies the objectives (skills) taught in the online learning product to the job.

Level 3 evaluation is cumbersome to do for classroom courses, because it requires time-consuming follow-up after the course. Computerization actually facilitates level 3 evaluation. Using something called push technology, a system can automatically send learners (and, if appropriate, their supervisors and co-workers) a note asking them to complete their level 3 evaluations. Polling software lets you automatically collect data, which can be exchanged with spreadsheets, where you can automatically interpret the data.

Level 4: Assessing Impact

Ultimately, a learning program not only changes the behavior of the learner in the long-run but also has an impact on the organization that sponsored the program. Level 4 evaluations attempt to measure that.

The most explicit level 4 evaluations are tied to the business objectives described in the sidebar earlier in this chapter. The measures that assess the extent to which a course met its business objectives almost always come from the sponsor's department and usually from a business report that the sponsor already generates. Therefore, you should work with the sponsor to get the data needed.

For example, suppose you were trying to assess whether learners met sales projections. You would work with the vice president of sales to assess the extent to which sales people who went through the online learning program met their sales objectives.

Note that outside business factors beyond learning can affect whether a learning program meets its business objectives, such as a change in staff or a change in the business environment. You should mention such factors that are known to affect the ability of an online learning program to meet its business objective when reporting level 4 evaluation results.

YOUR TURN

This chapter showed you how to set measurable objectives for your online learning program and explained why you prepare evaluations of those objectives now (before beginning design). Furthermore, you learned some pointers on how to apply the classic Kirkpatrick learning model to e-learning. Now think about a project you are working on, or expect to work on, and answer some questions on worksheet 4-1 to set your objectives and evaluation goals for an online learning program.

Worksheet 4-1. Setting learning and evaluation objectives for your e-learning project.

Content (Learning) Objectives

Terminal Objective 1: _____ (main task 1) _____
+ conditions + level of acceptable performance.

Enabling Objectives:

- _____ (supporting task 1) _____ + conditions + level of acceptable performance.

- _____

- _____

- _____

- _____

Terminal Objective 2: _____

Enabling Objectives:

- _____

- _____

- _____

- _____

Evaluation Objectives

- Have you prepared an evaluation form for level 1 (satisfaction)?

  ☐ Yes   ☐ No

- What type of level 2 (learning) evaluation have you prepared (base it on the content objectives)?

  ☐ Test (generating questions from the terminal objectives)

  ☐ Observation (generating a scenario from the terminal objectives)

- Have you prepared enough test questions or observations for each objective? (How many do you need for a test? For practice?)

  ☐ Yes   ☐ No

- What type of level 3 (transfer) evaluation do you plan to administer (base it on the content objectives)?

  ☐ Follow-up survey of learners, supervisors, and co-workers? If so, have you generated questions from the terminal objectives?

  ☐ Observation of learners in the workplace? If so, have you developed an observation checklist from the terminal and enabling objectives?

- How do you plan to assess level 4 (impact; base it on the business objective)? Specifically, which business measure from your sponsor do you plan to track?

5

Choosing the Right Format to Build Performance

How do you decide which e-learning approach will meet the needs of a particular organization facing a particular situation? This chapter explains how.

First, it presents a framework with which to consider the performance improvement challenge that you face, so you can choose the right combination of formal and informal learning products to address it. In doing so, you are challenged to expand your repertoire beyond the course or the manual. Next, this chapter explains how to choose the learning product that best meets the learning and technical requirements of the situation. After suggesting how to choose a type of learning product, this chapter explains how to identify and meet the expectations that learners bring to that type of product. Last, this chapter explains how to choose additional learning products that can ensure that learning occurs and is transferred to the job.

MOVING BEYOND THE TRADITIONAL TUTORIAL

Although moving courses from the classroom or a workbook into an online tutorial offers a way to quickly build an online learning product, it is only one of many options available to you. Tutorials are an example of a learning product that supports formal learning. Other products, such as Webzines, tips of the day, electronic coaches, online help, and online references, support informal learning. With your content objectives clearly stated and the evaluation objectives clearly identified, your first choice in the design process is which type of e-learning product to design.

WADING THROUGH A SEA OF CHOICES

Choosing a type of learning product involves balancing a variety of issues. Here are the key questions to ask:

■ *How will this content be used?* If the content is conceptual and intended for long-term retention by the learner, then you would choose a type of learning product that lets learners work through the content from beginning to end. If tracking or assessment is needed, the learning product should also let you assess the learning. If the content primarily consists of facts and figures to be used at the moment of need, then you would choose a type of learning product that directs learners to the information of interest as quickly as possible, without concern for prior learning, retention of the content, or assessment.

- *Are you designing for formal or informal learning?* If you are designing for formal learning, then your choices are primarily limited to learning products that let you track who's using the content and how well they're learning it. That way you can state objectives, partially or fully control a learner's path through the course, and assess the outcomes of the learning. If you are designing for informal learning, then you may choose a learning product that directs learners quickly to the content of interest, efficiently presents it, and then lets them use it. To maximize efficiency, you may just track hits to the Webpage rather than requiring individual enrollment. You would not formally assess learning because learners prescribe the objectives, not you. You may, however, provide learners with resources for assessing their own learning.

- *How much previous knowledge do learners have?* If learners have extensive prior knowledge, you can blend some learning products: formal for presenting, assessing, and tracking the acquisition of prescribed new knowledge; and informal to bring newcomers up to speed (unless you plan to conduct an entry test).

- *What is your preference?* Past history often plays a role in choosing types of learning products. For example, if you have the most experience developing courses and have no experience developing reference manuals, you might choose an online tutorial because it is the first one to come to mind.

- *What is the current format of the content?* When the content is already available as a tutorial or a reference, it is sometimes most efficient to leave the content in its current form but convert it to an online format.

- *What is the technology platform?* The technology platform that is currently in use within your organization sometimes restricts the types of learning products you can produce. In some instances, you do not have the tools needed to prepare certain types of learning products. For example, you may lack the software to produce animation. In other instances, learners' computers cannot display the program. For example, some organizations do not provide users with CD-ROM drives, much less DVD players. Other organizations restrict plug-ins (software used to play audio and video tracks) to improve network performance. Sometimes learners cannot download the necessary software because they connect over standard telephone lines. Others have limited software capabilities and cannot interpret certain types of programming instructions.

Managing Learners' Expectations

Learning products can be categorized into genres, just as movies and literature are. For example, when you see a comedy, you expect to laugh. If you don't laugh, you feel disappointed; if you see a romance and two people do not meet and fall in love, you feel cheated.

When choosing a type of communication product, you must not only match an appropriate type of product to the situation, but you must also identify the expectations that learners bring to it, and make sure that the product you design matches those expectations.

For example, people expect a tutorial to be based on a set of clearly stated learning objectives and to be written in a supportive style. Although many online tutorials let learners enter at various points, most learners expect the course to have definite starting and ending points, and offer a suggested path through the course.

These expectations also help learners effectively move through a learning product. For example, if you were to develop a user's guide, learners would know to check the table of contents or index to find topics of interest. You do not have to "teach" this content.

You must take these expectations into consideration when designing an e-learning product. Specifically, learners bring the following categories of expectations to each type of learning product:

- *The way that they will find information:* For example, people expect to go directly to information of interest in a reference, but to be led through the information in a tutorial.
- *Types of information available:* For example, people expect to find examples and exercises in a tutorial, but just the bare instructions in online help.
- *Format of information:* For example, people expect step-by-step procedures in help, whereas they expect to find product specifications and ordering options with catalog entries.
- *Writing style:* For example, people expect a direct writing style in references but a more supportive and colorful style in online demonstrations.
- *Screen design:* Certain types of learning products demand a certain type of presentation online. For example, tutorial screens usually fit the physical screen and usually do not require users to scroll. In contrast, Webzine articles usually extend beyond the length of the screen, but studies suggest that many users (though not all) will scroll down to read the rest of it. To encourage people to continue reading, many organizations include a mini-table of contents for the article at its beginning, with links to each of the subheadings.
- *Organization:* Different types of learning products follow different structures. For example, tutorials begin with objectives, follow with an introduction of the material, exercises, summary, and an assessment. In contrast, references follow alphabetic organization.

Meeting these expectations is an important part of winning learners' acceptance of online learning products.

TAKING A CAMPAIGN APPROACH TO LEARNING

Realistically, online learners are struggling with information overload, just as you are. They are bombarded with work-related messages from the Internet, intranet, email, voicemail, newsletters, mailings, and yellow Post-It notes. And, in many cases, they are given just brief breaks to study a topic. No wonder then that many can easily grasp the gist of a situation but have difficulty retaining specific facts when implementing the learning on the job (especially if implementation occurs much after the learning).

No problem: An online learning program need not be designed as a single course intended as a one-time event. Instead, you can design it as a campaign for ongoing support of learners as they apply their learning in the workplace.

A campaign consists of a variety of learning products, each intended to develop skills at a different stage of the learning development process. See table 5-1 for the stages of the performance cycle during which learners need support.

MASTER LIST OF E-LEARNING PRODUCTS

What follows is an alphabetic list of the most common delivery vehicles for e-learning. Detailed descriptions of these forms of e-learning follow. Also check the Website for this book (http://saulcarliner.home.att.net/oll/index.html) for links to examples of many of these forms. These examples are provided online because many involve several screens and user interaction. The most common delivery vehicles are the following:

- advertisements
- celebrations
- classes
- coaches and advisors
- contests
- cue cards
- demos (guided tours)
- frequently asked questions (FAQs)
- gaming simulations
- help
- job aids and quick references
- newsletters and Webzines
- online references
- specialized troubleshooting procedures
- support groups (online communities)
- tip of the day
- tutorials
- wizards.

Each of these learning products is described in some detail in the sections that follow. Each section includes a description of the learning product, situations in which learners consult the particular type of learning product, types of learning supported, what learners expect in this type of learning product, communication style, and examples of the learning product.

Table 5-1. Tailoring your offerings to the stage in the learning development process.

Stage in the Learning Development Process	Learning Product Suggestions
Advance Notice	Learners benefit from products that build motivation to learn the concept or technical subject. Informal learning products whose objectives are primarily affective (motivational) work best. These include brief demonstrations (guided tours), preview articles in newsletters, and "advertisements" of the concept. If some learners have previous experience, self-assessments help them gauge the extent of their prior knowledge and build their confidence in transferring skills.
Getting Started	This is the time when learners are trying out a skill or concept for the first time. Motivation to learn is high, but so is apprehension. Formal learning products that are focused on developing first-day performance (that is, getting people to perform something useful on the first day and shielding users from unnecessary choice) are useful. Informal learning products—that are introduced in the formal class—serve as reminders back on the job.
Feeling Arrogant	Intermediate users who have mastered the basic skills and now want to improve their efficiency and effectiveness can be affectionately called "arrogant" because they often become a bit overconfident in their skills at this phase, unaware of what they do not know. A combination of formal and informal learning products helps learners at this phase. Short tutorials introduce learners to what they can do; help and other informal types of products provide instructions.
Feeling Humble	These are advanced users, who are ready to tackle content that might not even be documented yet. I affectionately refer to learners at this level as "humble" because, although they are extremely proficient with the basic and intermediate skills, they are usually aware of the limits of their knowledge. Informal learning products that let learners interact with other experts are most helpful at this level.

ADVERTISEMENTS

Description
Promotions of various aspects of a product or service. Often appears inside the front or back covers of a publication or on the screens displayed by an application when users start or install it.

Situations in Which Learners Consult This Type of Product
Learners do not consult this type of information; they receive it while performing other activities.

Types of Learning Supported
- Informal
- Advance notice (by building enthusiasm for the topic)
- "Feeling arrogant" (by making learners aware of possibilities available to them)

What Learners Expect in This Type of Learning Product

- To be "sold" to
- A certain level of hyperbole

Communication Style

- Catchy, to gain and hold attention of users
- Focused on benefits (that is, how the learning or concept can help learners work more efficiently or effectively, or comply with regulations, rather than what the learning is)
- Persuasive
- Clever
- Heavily visual rather than verbal

Examples

- Pop-up messages received about a product as it installs on a hard drive
- Email reminders sent to potential learners about an e-learning course
- Banner advertising on Websites

CELEBRATIONS

Description

Ceremonies and observances intended to recognize work with online learning and build morale around it. This type of recognition is especially important to online learning, because the learning is often anonymous. A celebration may be as simple as a supervisor telling an employee that he or she is aware of the worker's participation in a course or presenting a ribbon or plaque to acknowledge achievement, or a celebration may be as elaborate as a party.

Situations in Which Learners Consult This Type of Product

When learners' feelings play a key role in the acceptance of new products, policies, procedures, or ideas and when many of those learners can be gathered in a single place at one time.

Types of Learning Supported

- Informal
- "Getting started"
- "Feeling arrogant"
- "Feeling humble" (by recognizing achievements)

What Learners Expect in This Type of Learning Product

- To receive personal attention and recognition
- To enjoy themselves

■ To be in a nonthreatening atmosphere

■ To participate in a formal ceremony such as a speech

Communication Style

■ Festive (including food and beverages)

■ Inoffensive

■ Inclusive

■ Soft-sell approach, never a hard sell

Examples

■ Certificate issued at the end of courses

■ Luncheon for learners who complete a course

■ Prizes for those who complete a course

CLASSES

Description

A lesson, or series of lessons, that is intended to develop a skill that users can immediately use. The lessons are taken synchronously. That is, the learners interact online with an instructor who is online at the same time. A transcript of the learning session might be available for later use.

Situations in Which Learners Consult This Type of Product

■ When taking a for-credit course

■ When taking courses designed for extensive interaction with other students and the instructor

■ When hearing a guest speaker

Types of Learning Supported

■ Formal

■ All levels from "getting started" to "feeling humble"

What Learners Expect in This Type of Learning Product

■ As in a traditional classroom, learners expect that an instructor will facilitate the session.

■ At the beginning of the session, learners expect an overview of the session.

■ During the session, learners expect a combination of learning activities, such as lectures, exercises, and discussion.

■ Learners expect to be able to interrupt the instructor to ask a question and to have their attention held throughout the session.

■ If the session exceeds 90 minutes, learners expect a break.

- Learners expect that the Internet connection will remain active through the entire session.
- At the end of the session, learners expect the instructor to present a summary of key points.

Communication Style

- Speaking in a supportive tone and language, using a combination of word choice and tone to subtly communicate to learners that they can master the material
- Asserting the instructor's control of the class
- Receiving clear instructions from the instructor
- Segmenting the session like a television show rather than like a class. Endless lecture anesthetizes students in a classroom, but it kills learners in online classrooms. To avoid the droning lecture, segment the class into a series of seven- to 10-minute segments, each using a different mode of teaching. If the first segment is lecture, the second might involve an exercise.
- Presenting an image of the instructor. If your system cannot Webcast a video image, then include a photograph of the instructor that is visible at all times; learners want to see their instructor.
- Displaying PowerPoint slides and other visuals during the class

Examples

- Distance learning at Bentley College in Waltham, Massachusetts. Students participate in courses taught synchronously online (http://atc.bentley.edu/de /classes.html).
- Distance education degrees from the University of Phoenix Online (http://www.universityofphoenixonline.com/). Students participate in asynchronous learning in a format that resembles email.

COACHES AND ADVISORS

Description

Online tools that assist users with cognitive (intellectual) tasks. Usually, the coaching instructions are built into the software, but sometimes, the coach is an actual person who interacts with a learner through instant messaging.

Situations in Which Learners Consult This Type of Product

- Learners must make a decision and seek rapid access to expert advice, often when they have little time for extensive "teaching."
- The organization believes that the advice of experts can be coded into a program to enable workers with less experience to make informed decisions.

Types of Learning Supported

- Informal
- "Advance notice" (by building enthusiasm for the topic)
- "Feeling arrogant" (by making learners aware of possibilities available to them)

What Learners Expect in This Type of Product

- Partial or full assistance with the decision
- Prompting with scripts to be read when appropriate

Communication Style

- Empathetic
- Didactic (explanatory), including concepts
- To the point and brief
- Interactive; for the system to assist with decisions, it needs as complete information as possible
- Links to other programs, such as databases, as appropriate

Examples

- Mavis Beacon Teaches Typing
- Quicken Credit Assessment (at www.quicken.com)
- Advisors at e-commerce sites, such as Travelocity.com and quicken.com, who take and respond to users' questions through instant messaging
- Online assistants that tell customer service representatives at credit card companies whether or not they can extend a customer's credit limit
- Online tools that help workers choose a personalized curriculum of training courses

CONTESTS

Description

Motivational tool intended to build interest or attention to a subject. For example, an organization might run a contest that rewards a department for reaching certain levels of safety or for levels of usage for a new computer system.

Situations in Which Learners Consult This Type of Product

Meaningful incentives encourage participation in contests.

Types of Learning Supported

- Informal
- "Getting started" (by providing an incentive for reaching basic levels of performance)
- "Feeling arrogant" (by providing an incentive for reaching intermediate levels of performance)

What Learners Expect in This Type of Learning Product
- Prize
- Rules for winning the prize
- A fair shot at winning

Communication Style
- Clear instructions
- Motivational message to join

Examples
- A game that accompanies a course, such as "Let's Make a Respiratory Deal" for a course on biological systems
- Incentives for completing a course, such as providing a t-shirt to learners for enrolling in an e-learning course by a certain date or providing certificates to a coffee house for the first 100 learners who complete the course

---

CUE CARDS

Description
Instructions that tell learners how to perform a task and that are displayed by the system one step at a time. These instructional aids resemble flash or cue cards, from which they receive their name.

Situations in Which Learners Consult This Type of Product
When they are not familiar with a procedure but want to learn it, as might be the case the first time a learner has performed a given procedure or the first time the user has performed the procedure after a long intervening period.

Types of Learning Supported
- Informal (when standalone)
- Formal (when integrated into a tutorial)
- Follow-up for "getting started" learning
- Supportive learning for those who are "feeling arrogant"

What Learners Expect in This Type of Product
- Step-by-step instructions
- One instruction at a time
- Simultaneous display of the instruction and the software in which users perform it

Communication Style
- Terse, direct
- No explanatory language (except, perhaps, in an opening cue card that provides an overview of the procedure)
- Assistance with decision making

Examples
- Cue cards included in Microsoft Access
- Electronic flash cards used in e-learning programs like math and geography, which primarily teach rote memorization skills

DEMOS (GUIDED TOURS)

Description
A trial version of a product that provides users with a "tour" of the product. The tour may be guided, or it may be self-running. In some instances, demos provide users with an opportunity to try certain aspects of a product.

Situations in Which Learners Consult This Type of Product
- When they are first using a concept or technical subject and want to "survey the landscape" before plunging into the entire learning process
- When people are considering purchasing a product

Types of Learning Supported
- Informal
- Formal (with low-level learning objectives, primarily related to recognition)
- "Advance notice"

What Learners Expect in This Type of Product
- High-level information, rather than operating details
- Suggestions of how users can use the product in their own lives

Communication Style
- Persuasive
- Visual, primarily pictures with a few words of explanation
- Focused on benefits rather than features

Examples
- The quick tour offered on Hello Brain (www.hellobrain.com)
- Demo program for the master's of hospitality management course at the Conrad N. Hilton College of Hotel and Restaurant Management (http://www.mhmonline.uh.edu/demo.htm)

FREQUENTLY ASKED QUESTIONS (FAQs)

Description

A list of questions about a subject that provides learners with quick answers about issues that arise in their use of software, Website, or a general subject area. The questions are either ones that the authors anticipated, or come from an analysis of the questions that learners ask. Usually, the list of questions is a visible link from a Website. The first thing learners see is the list of questions. Learners choose a question of interest and then see the answer.

Situations in Which Learners Consult This Type of Product

- When questions arise while using software or a Website
- When encountering a new topic

Types of Learning Supported

Informal, especially those who are "getting started" without the benefit of formal learning and those who are "feeling arrogant," but wondering "what if" or running into problems.

What Learners Expect in This Type of Product

- A list of questions presented first, with links to their answers
- Direct answers to questions
- A minimal number of cross-references (links to more in-depth explanations)

Communication Style

- Interrogative
- Direct
- Supportive, but not likely to lead to misinterpretations of the answers

Examples

- FAQ at the Website for Dell Computer technical support, which lists the problems that people most frequently call about
- FAQ at eBay.com

GAMING SIMULATIONS

Description

Learning experiences that replicate the central characteristics of complex situations (that's the simulation) and allow users to experience the consequences of decisions made in that situation (the gaming aspect).

Situations in Which Learners Consult This Type of Product
- When the actual situation could place the learner and others in harm's way
- When learners need to experience a situation in its entirety rather than components of the situation

Types of Learning Supported
- Formal
- All levels, especially "feeling arrogant" and "feeling humble" situations in which experience can serve as a powerful learning tool

What Learners Expect in This Type of Product
- Realism
- As few instructions as possible
- Opportunities to make real decisions
- Opportunities to learn about the consequences of different possible decisions in given situations

Communication Style
- Realistic
- Interactive
- Appropriate to the situation
- Includes a debriefing, in which users can reflect on the situation, learn the essential elements of the model presented, reinforce good decisions, and avoid bad ones

Examples
- SimCity 3000 computer game
- Aircraft and nuclear simulators, which provide "practice disasters" for pilots and operators in training
- Training courses in interpersonal relations, such as sales and management

---

HELP

Description
A special type of user's guide for software that is available to users online as they use software applications.

Situations in Which Learners Consult This Type of Product
- Before starting a task to find out whether it is possible to perform and, if so, how to perform it
- In the middle of performing a task, for a reminder of how to complete it
- After performing a task, to explain unanticipated results

Users can access information in help via the following:

- Table of contents, which lists the major sections within help
- "Search for help on," which acts like an index in that it lets users type in the term they seek information about, then displays all of the index entries that mention that term
- Index, which lets users scan through the entire index
- Links (also called hyperlinks), which let users jump directly from one topic to a related one by clicking on a highlighted term

Type of Learning Supported

- Formal, when serving as a primary means of building additional skills for "feeling arrogant" and "feeling humble" learners
- Informal, when serving as a reminder to "getting started," "feeling arrogant," and "feeling humble" learners who have seen the material before but want exact content as support

What Learners Expect in This Type of Product

- Assistance with a task or using software—a high level of expectation when the system cannot interrogate the user
- "What's this?" help, which explains the various elements of a screen and tells users how to respond
- "How do I?" help, which provides step-by-step instructions for performing tasks
- Examples and demonstrations, which shows users how to perform specific tasks and the likely results
- Tips and techniques to acquaint users quickly with aspects of the software they might not have otherwise noticed
- Cue cards, which display, one instruction at a time, the instructions for performing tasks
- Wizards, which automatically perform tasks for users, except for those parts in which users must make choices
- Access to online tutorials
- "Stay-on-top help," which keeps instructions visible to users as they perform the task

Communication Style

Much like that of a user's guide. Because the information is displayed online, however, make generous use of visuals as long as they meet organizational limits on the size of help files.

Examples

- Click on help button in any Windows or Macintosh application
- Microsoft Office Assistant

JOB AIDS AND QUICK REFERENCES

Description
A learning product intended to give users a brief refresher of a training module on the job. Job aids also go by the name *quick references.*

Situations in Which Learners Consult This Type of Product
- In the middle of a task
- When they need a quick reminder about a key point

Type of Learning Supported
- Informal, for all types of learners

What Learners Expect in This Type of Product
- To contain cryptic, but meaningful, reminders

Communication Style
- Terse, almost to the point of seeming incomplete.

Examples
- Reminders, such as reminders about appointments sent by Microsoft Outlook
- Quick references and "look-up" software, such as the link to calendars and airport codes at travel sites

NEWSLETTERS AND WEBZINES

Description
Contain a collection of articles and provide ongoing communication with a target group. For example, a product newsletter or Webzine provides ongoing contact with the customers who have already purchased a product. An employee newsletter or Webzine provides ongoing contact with the employees in a department or within an entire organization. Generally, organizations distribute online newsletters through email and publish Webzines at specific Websites.

Situations in Which Learners Consult This Type of Product
- Users usually receive newsletters or link to the Webzine when they pick up their email; they might skim the publication at that time and, if they see any interesting articles, read the articles at a later time.
- Generally, users read in depth those articles that help them address an immediate need or provide them with a much-needed skill.

Type of Learning Supported

- Informal
- For "getting started" learners, models of successful mastery of the skills
- For "feeling arrogant" learners, makes them aware of additional skills they can master
- For "feeling humble" learners, makes them aware of undocumented techniques

What Learners Expect in This Type of Product

- A newsletter or Webzine for the primary purpose of maintaining contact with existing customers can suggest additional ways of using existing products, highlight new products, and, if customers have contact with the staff, offer profiles of people whom customers might deal with.
- A newsletter or Webzine that is supported by a technical support group can provide answers to FAQs, tell users about new software available to them, and provide profiles of the members of the technical support team.
- For all newsletters, learners expect regular placement of certain information. For example, many newsletters and Webzines have links to the regular editorial "departments" on the navigation bar to the right and place a link to columnists (if any) in the upper right corner. Most have a link to a page called "About," which provides the same type of information in a masthead of a printed newsletter or magazine. Learners who want this information immediately turn to it.

Communication Style

- A persuasive, informative style
- Second person
- Adherence to organizational style and editorial guidelines, as well as basic rules of grammar

Examples

- ASTD's *Learning Circuits* (http://www.learningcircuits.org/)
- Jacob Nielsen's column on usability (www.useit.com)
- *Online Learning e-News* (www.vnulearning.com)

ONLINE REFERENCES

Description

Encylopedic listings of all major topics on particular subjects, including online versions of standard references (telephone directories, encyclopedias, specialty dictionaries and glossaries, and so forth). Also included in this category are software programming references, which list all the commands that programmers can use to create their own applications using that software, and similar types of technical references.

Situations in Which Learners Consult This Type of Product

To look up specific piece of information. The subject might be broad, such as all the commands used for copying information or all the medications used to treat influenza. The subject might be tightly defined, such as the use of global characters with the DOS command, diskcopy, or the side effects of a certain influenza vaccine on patients with pacemakers. Users generally do not read references in their entirety.

Type of Learning Supported

- Informal
- "Feeling arrogant" or "feeling humble" learners whenever they need to look up a fact or small piece of information that relates to something they already know

What Learners Expect in This Type of Product

- Comprehensive coverage of a subject, with every major topic listed and thorough descriptions within each. For example, if a programming language has 118 commands, learners expect listings for each. If doctors have access to 1,089 drugs, they expect their online formulary to describe all 1,089 of them.
- Alphabetic listing
- Examples and illustrations to explain concepts
- Programming references should include a description of the command, a diagram showing the syntax of the command, a description of each parameter and the options available for each parameter, a comprehensive discussion of considerations for use, and examples of commands that handle particular situations.

Communication Style

Direct, explanatory, and terse. In fact, references often use sentence fragments and lists to present information. References generally do not give step-by-step procedures; designers expect learners to integrate the information and determine for themselves how to use it. Designers expect users of most technical references to have a certain level of technical expertise and use technical terminology. However, because terms might be unfamiliar to many users, communicators also provide definitions of the terms, at the least, within a sentence and, at the most, in a glossary.

Examples

- Material safety data sheets for safe chemical use (http://msds.pdc.cornell.edu/msdssrch.asp)
- *E-Learning Glossary* (http://www.learningcircuits.org/glossary.html)
- *AVP Virus Encyclopedia* (www.virusdatabase.com)

SPECIALIZED TROUBLESHOOTING PROCEDURES

Description

A special type of instruction manual that tells trained service representatives how to repair a piece of equipment, resolve a problem with software, or handle some similar type of problem. Service representatives usually receive training in how to use troubleshooting procedures. The troubleshooting guide for a computer is an example of a service guide.

Types of Learning Supported

- Formal and informal, as well as nonlearning (if the procedures are self-running)
- Used in conjunction with "getting started" education for training in how to use the procedures
- Used by "feeling arrogant" and "feeling humble" learners to extend their skills

Situations in Which Learners Consult This Type of Product

Online references are usually consulted under challenging circumstances. Users have usually tried, without success, to resolve the problem on their own. The broken equipment or the nonfunctioning software usually brings the client's business to a standstill. Therefore, clients are usually anxious for the service representative to resolve the problem as quickly as possible.

What Learners Expect in This Type of Product

- Procedures helping them to isolate the problem and, once isolated, instructions on how to fix the problem. Learners do not expect explanations of the problem; most of them have sufficient technical knowledge to determine that on their own.
- Illustrations, if they would be useful in isolating and resolving the problem. For example, learners working with a hardware service guide might appreciate illustrations of the parts of the hardware, so that they can match the parts they see with their names and purposes.
- Many such learning products use unique formats that are not, on first glance, intuitive, but have proven extremely effective with their users. To make most effective use of this training, many organizations follow a standard format for all troubleshooting procedures.

Communication Style

- Directive writing style that extensively uses technical terminology

Examples

- Troubleshooting Windows XP (http://www.windowshelp.net/WindowsXP/troub-idx.html)
- Troubleshooting a computer mouse (http://www.users.bigpond.com/billimetzke/PC_Maintenance-Cleaning.htm#mouse)

SUPPORT GROUPS (ONLINE COMMUNITIES)

Description

Groups of people facing a similar challenge and who benefit from sharing individual problems. Some online communities are self-run, and others are led by outside facilitators. Some support groups are available online as discussion listservs and newsgroups. Some support groups meet in person at formal users' meetings.

Situations in Which Learners Consult This Type of Product

- When using complex technical content, for which the documentation and training are incomplete
- When handling complex interpersonal situations

Type of Learning Supported

- Formal (in the sense that participants learn from one another)
- Informal (in the sense that they have no formal agenda)
- "Getting started" and "feeling arrogant" learning, by providing for validation and alternative explanations
- "Feeling humble" learning, by providing a forum for answering undocumented questions

What Learners Expect in This Type of Product

- Compassionate facilitator
- Open format that allows each person to describe problems (if any)
- Regular meetings
- Confidentiality
- Opportunity to learn from others "in the same boat"

Communication Style Used

- Live
- Online "chats" or other form of synchronous connection
- Asynchronous discussion listservs, which may or may not have moderators who keep the discussion going and scan posts to prevent conversations from going off-topic or degenerating into arguments

Examples

- Discussion boards on EPSS InfoSite (www.epssinfosite.com)
- ASTD's online communities (www.astd.org)

TIP OF THE DAY

Description

A suggestion about some aspect of software or a subject area that is not required for basic use or application, but the knowledge thereof could increase the productivity of the user.

Situations in Which Learners Consult This Type of Product

- At the beginning of the day (or when the user starts the program or checks email)
- As a refresher (the user originally may have received the tip at a time when it wasn't needed but now has that need)

Types of Learning Supported

- Informal
- "Feeling humble," by providing learners with information about ways to develop their skills

What Learners Expect in This Type of Learning Product

- Brief
- Limited to a single topic at time
- Covers a broad range of issues over a period of time
- Primarily covers procedural topics
- Introduction of a concept
- Lets learners turn off tips
- Allows users to refer back to tips

Communication Style

- Terse, no more than three to five lines of text
- Answers the question "Did you know?"
- Provides instructions if they are brief (no more than two or three steps)
- Refers learners to appropriate sources for instructions that exceed two or three steps
- Is tailored to the needs of different learners
- Can be transferred to a scratch pad where learners can copy relevant tips for future reference

Examples

- Opening screens of Microsoft Outlook and Quicken
- HTML tip of the day (http://html.miningco.com/library/bl_tipaday.htm)

TUTORIALS

Description

A lesson, or series of lessons, which are intended to develop a skill that users can immediately use. The lessons are taken asynchronously; that is, all of the learning content is available online. Learners can take it at their convenience.

Situations in Which Learners Consult This Type of Product

Learners embark on tutorials for a variety of reasons. In some instances, they're told to. For example, employees may be required to take training about a new company policy or to fulfill a legal requirement (the reason for most safety training). In some instances, learners take tutorials to learn how to perform a task in a more instructive way than might be found in a procedure manual or online help. Examples include learners consulting commercial books about software, such as *Windows XP for Dummies,* to learn how to back up systems and tutorials provided with spreadsheets that teach users how to use formulas. In other instances, learners take tutorials to learn about an entire subject, such as tutorials on CD-ROM about career management and workbooks about preparing taxes.

Types of Learning Supported

- Formal
- All levels of learners

What Learners Expect in This Type of Product

At the beginning of a lesson, users expect

- A brief description of the purpose of the lesson (about 30 to 50 words)
- A list of skills users will develop (take them directly from your content objectives)
- Prerequisite skills and knowledge
- Length of time needed for the lesson, so they can decide whether they have sufficient time now or if they need to take the lesson later

During the lesson, users expect

- Clear explanations of concepts and procedures
- Practical examples of the skills
- Opportunities to apply the new skills
- Active involvement in the learning process through exercises, simulations, questions, and other techniques

At the end of the lesson, users expect

- Descriptive summary that repeats the main points they should remember
- Glossary, which defines new technical terms presented in the tutorial

Learners expect the following material in a tutorial:

- Running headers and footers
- Forward and backward buttons to let them reread information they have already seen
- In some instances, learners prefer that you recommend a sequence through the tutorial and do not give them alternative methods of going through it. In other instances, learners prefer to have total control over their movement through the tutorial.

Communication Style

The writing style for tutorials is persuasive because the tutorial needs to motivate users to take an interest in the subject matter. The writing style must also be clear and involving so learners understand the material presented, see how it relates to them, and feel actively involved in the lesson. Finally, the style should be polite, though direct, like that of a good teacher with a student.

Examples

- Mavis Beacon Teaches Typing
- Courses from DigitalThink, SmartForce, or Wilson Learning
- Courses from EEI Communications (http://www.eeicommunications.com /training/classes.html)

WIZARDS

Description

Online "agents" that automatically perform complex tasks for learners, only prompting learners when they must make a decision. When learners are prompted to make decisions, the system should have a default (presumed) choice to offer.

Situations in Which Learners Consult This Type of Product

- To perform once-in-a-lifetime or similarly rare tasks
- To perform tasks that intimidate users

Types of Learning Supported

- "Nonlearning," because the system performs the task
- "Getting started" learners
- Tasks that "feeling humble" learners do not need to perform frequently

What Learners Expect in This Type of Product
- To be shielded from the complexity of the process
- To make simple decisions within their realm of knowledge, such as entering their name or choosing the style of the finished product
- A limited number of steps (no more than 10)
- Well-chosen defaults

Communication Style
- When presenting instructions, use directive language ("Do this")
- When presenting choices, use a therapist's sensitivity ("Would you prefer...") rather than "You should..."
- Use only plain language; avoid technical terminology unless absolutely necessary or the audience has the training to understand it

Examples
- Wizards for installing software on a PC
- Online reservation systems, such as Travelocity (www.Travelocity.com) and Orbitz (www.orbitz.com)

YOUR TURN

This chapter gave you a great deal of choice among the learning products you can use to create effective e-learning. Consider a project you are currently working on or expect to work on and use the exercises in worksheet 5-1 to help narrow down your choices.

Worksheet 5-1. Narrow the field of e-learning vehicles for your project.

With online learning products, you can choose among a variety of types of learning products to serve a specific set of needs.

Type of Learning Product	Check one:
	☐ Advertisements
	☐ Celebrations
	☐ Classes
	☐ Coaches and advisors
	☐ Contests
	☐ Cue cards
	☐ Demos (guided tours)
	☐ FAQs
	☐ Gaming simulations
	☐ Help
	☐ Job aids (quick references)
	☐ Newsletters and Webzines
	☐ Online references
	☐ Specialized troubleshooting procedures
	☐ Support groups (online communities)
	☐ Tip of the day
	☐ Tutorials
	☐ Wizards
Why did you choose this type of product?	_____
How do people find information in this type of product?	_____
What type of information do learners expect to find?	_____
What is the expected format of the information?	_____
What is the appropriate communication style?	_____

6

Designing the Content, Part 1: Developing a High-Level Concept

Until now, the design process has focused on what content to present. Now, attention turns to the challenge of how to present it. You addressed part of this challenge in the last phase, when you determined the format that the learning content should take.

The heart of this challenge is in design, one of the most complex activities of the entire design and development process because, in this activity, you actually plan the presentation of the content. Design for an e-learning project really involves two levels of design and related documentation:

- *high-level, or conceptual, design:* A high-level design is a general strategy for presenting the material in the learning program. It involves structuring the content and preparing a strategy for presenting it. Developing a high-level design in many ways is the most complex phase of the entire design and development process because you actually plan the presentation of the content.
- *detailed design:* A detailed design fleshes out the high-level design with specific plans for presenting all of the content. These specific plans include a prototype section, the general design of screens, and storyboards for all content not covered in the sample section. You also conduct a usability test on the prototype, a special type of pilot test that also tests the ease with which learners can use the software. Chapter 7 discusses detailed design.
- *guidelines and templates for the project:* These guidelines record issues regarding editorial and visual consistency of the content, technical specifications, schedules, budgets, and staff. Chapter 8 discusses the development of guidelines and templates.

This chapter explores the first of these activities: high-level design. It begins with a general discussion about the principles of adult learning, then explains how to structure the content, and finally offers suggestions for preparing a strategy for presenting the content.

APPLYING THE SEVEN "BYTES" OF ADULT LEARNING THEORY TO E-LEARNING

One of the great challenges of designing learning programs—whether online or in the classroom—is designing them so people really learn from them. Focusing the content, clearly identifying the audience, and describing the learning context as you did in the needs analysis are essential to this goal. In addition, keep in mind some general characteristics of adult learners, which also shape the learning experience.

Byte 1: Adult Learning Is Andragogy, not Pedagogy

Andragogy, a term popularized by Malcolm Knowles (1988), refers to the art and science of teaching adults. Andragogy encompasses principles that instructional designers must address when preparing learning programs for adults. Pedagogy, on the other hand, refers to the art and science of teaching children, whose learning needs differ significantly from those of adults.

Byte 2: Adult Learners Are Pressed for Time

Adults squeeze in learning between demanding jobs, family responsibilities, and community commitments. Even with a high motivation for learning, the call of life limits the time that many adults can invest in learning. Adults who must balance demanding work and home lives benefit from the any time, any place convenience of e-learning. In fact, they comprise one of its primary markets.

Byte 3: Adult Learners Are Goal-Oriented

Adults primarily participate in learning programs to achieve a particular goal. The goal may be work-related such as using a computer system more effectively or writing a performance plan that conforms to company guidelines. Or, perhaps the learning goal is personal, such as the desire to learn basic Japanese in advance of a vacation in Japan or learning PhotoShop to prepare a family Website.

Classroom trainers often begin courses by asking how learners hope to benefit from a course and may tailor their content accordingly. That's not possible with asynchronous e-courses, so e-learning designers must perform a strong needs analysis to anticipate those needs.

Byte 4: Adult Learners Bring Previous Knowledge and Experience

In some cases, learners already know some or all of the content. Many time-pressed adult learners prefer not to review that content again. Through e-learning, instructional designers can first assess what learners already know and let them skip familiar material.

In some instances, an instructional designer can tie new material to learners' existing knowledge and experience, and create a more powerful and relevant learning experience. In other instances, the learning program contradicts material that people previously encountered. In such situations, instructional designers must first convince learners to part with the old approach before learners can grasp the new.

In other instances, asynchronous e-learning puts the instructional designer at a disadvantage because the designer cannot directly interact with learners to find out what they already know and tailor content accordingly. The same issues arise in synchronous e-learning unless the instructional designer makes a concerted effort to integrate learners in other locations into the course discussion and actively seeks their input.

Byte 5: Information Overload is Real

Consider all of the passwords that you use in a given day. You may have one for your computer, one for your voicemail system at work, and another for your voicemail system at home. You have a password for your automatic teller machine, the cipher lock at work, the locker at the gym, and your online banking account. That's a lot of passwords to remember, but, admittedly, human long-term memory has an infinite capacity.

Nevertheless, everything stored in long-term memory must first go through short-term memory, and that has a constrained capacity. As a result, people can only learn so much at a given moment.

Ever-increasing storage capacities on computers provide designers and developers of online learning programs with little incentive to curb the quantity of information presented in courses. It is important to remember, though, that the capacity of human short-term memory is fixed at five to nine items. To increase the likelihood that learners will retain content, instructional designers must avoid overloading learners.

One way to avoid overloading learners is by asking them to memorize only the most significant material. Learners just need to know where to find the less essential material when they need it. Even better, eliminate material that learners do not really need to know to avoid overloading learners. Conversely, repeating content that learners must know helps reinforce the learning.

Byte 6: Adult Learners Have Different Motivation Levels

During the first six weeks to three months on a job, adults are highly motivated to learn. When faced with a new work process or approach, adults are similarly motivated to learn. (What stifles their motivation, at this point, is fear of failure and difficulty in "unlearning" old habits.) The motivation to learn also changes as learners become more acquainted with the subject.

Getting Started Stage. During this stage, as described in chapter 5, the learner's primary learning goal is getting started—learning enough material to proficiently handle the routine tasks. Learners only need how-to instruction and supervision at this point. Formal e-learning is primarily appropriate at this phase.

Too often, however, instructional designers provide learners with more content than they need at this point. For example, rather than telling users how to power on the system unit and start the word-processing program, most of the early computer training for end users taught the history of computers, the intricacies of random access memory, and elements of DOS. Rather than deepening learners' understanding, this material only confused and intimidated them.

"Feeling Arrogant" Stage. At this stage of learning, learners have mastered routine tasks and gained confidence. They want to learn how to handle routine tasks more efficiently and how to handle some of the less common tasks. Learners still want instruction at this point, but some do not want supervision or practice. Because they better understand the subject, learners also know more specifically the skills they would like to develop. In this stage, motivation to participate in formal learning wanes, so a combination of formal and informal e-learning is helpful.

"Feeling Humble" Stage. At this stage, learners' motivation wanes further. Primary learning goals are handling undocumented situations. In situations like these, learning usually happens informally, one expert to another; learners appreciate discussion groups and other less formal learning programs whereby they can research answers to their specific questions.

Byte 7: Adult Learners Have Different Learning Styles

Some people prefer to "do" first and pick up content through trial-and-error. Then—through a debriefing process—they put labels on the ideas covered and learn how to apply those concepts more broadly. Other people prefer to "learn" everything first, then perform a task, reducing the likelihood of errors when trying something for the first time. Neither approach is entirely right. They simply represent different learners' approaches to learning.

In addition to the do-then-learn versus the learn-then-do styles, another set of learning styles pertains to the sense through which a learner best responds. Some learners are verbal learners and learn best by reading. Other learners are visual learners and learn best by seeing. Auditory learners learn best by hearing, and kinesthetic learners learn best by touch (hands-on experience).

In an ideal world, each learning program would be able to accommodate the different learning styles of all the learners. Learners would more likely master the content because they learn in their preferred style.

Despite the promise that e-learning can address different learning styles, the practical reality requires that designers plan and develop separate versions of a learning program for each learning style (for example, a visual version of a learning program as well as a verbal version). Because that's not usually feasible, designers try to account for the variety of learning styles by using a variety of strategies to present content throughout a learning program. Over the course of an entire learning program, then, most learners' styles will ideally have been addressed once.

For example, one section of a course might be more visual than verbal, another might include an audio track, and still another might include a hands-on exercise. Although the entire learning program does not focus on one learning style, learners with each style will find some content specifically geared toward their needs.

Prepare the High-Level Design

With these issues of adult learning in mind, you are ready to begin preparing a high-level design. A high-level design is the general strategy for presenting the content in the learning program. Through it, you structure the learning program into sections and determine an overall strategy for presenting material in each.

Structure the Content

When structuring the content, you essentially do three things. First, you impose an "order" onto the information, determining which information appears first, which appears next, and so forth. Second, you divide the content into sections. Sometimes, you divide the content further into subsections. Third, you consider the elements that are part of every e-learning program but do not appear in a listing of the content. These elements include title pages, menus, and glossaries. Specifically, consider the following six issues when structuring the content.

Consider the General Structure of an E-Learning Program. In addition to its basic content, every published work online or in print follows a certain structure. Each begins with certain elements (called front matter) and ends with other ones (called back matter). See chapter 11 for more detailed information on how to create front and back matter.

Essentially, the front matter for an entire learning program includes the title screen, main menu, edition notice, preface, and instructions. The back matter for an entire learning program includes a course exam (if any), index, glossary, and a level 1 (satisfaction) form.

Each unit (lesson) in your learning program also should have front and back matter associated with it. The front matter for a specific unit may include

- an introductory screen, which lists the title of the lesson, as well as its objectives, prerequisite skills and resources, and estimated time (might require two screens)
- a menu of topics within the unit.

The back matter for a specific unit may include the following:

- descriptive summary, which reviews both the topics covered and the points learners should remember about them
- assessment of learning, which could be an informal quiz or a formal test
- list of additional resources, which can help learners can find additional information about the topic
- job aids to be used by learners on the job.

For example, consider figures 6-1 and 6-2, which are introductory and summary screens from an online course about newsletter editing.

Develop an Overall Structure for the Content. With the general outline of an online learning program in mind (as well as the general outline of a lesson), you next determine how to structure the content within the course and within individual lessons.

The first thing you do is develop overall schemes for the course and each lesson. One large chunk of that work is already finished: the content (learning) objectives tell you what content should be presented, the hierarchy of that content, and the order in which the points should be presented if learners go through the content in linear fashion. Online learners typically do not follow this strategy, so you also need to present the structure of the content in such a way that learners can easily find the material they

Figure 6-1. An introductory screen for an online course.

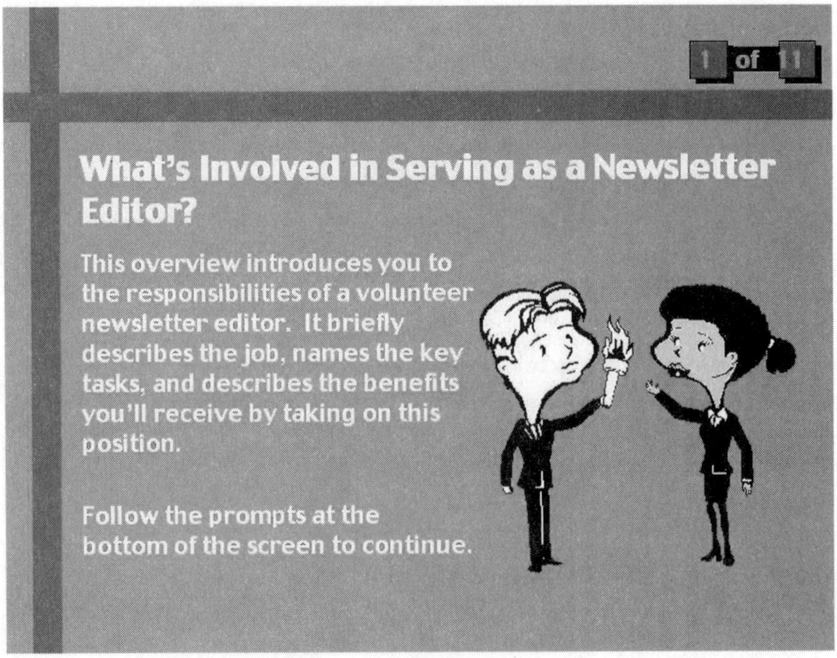

Figure 6-2. Summary screens for an online course.

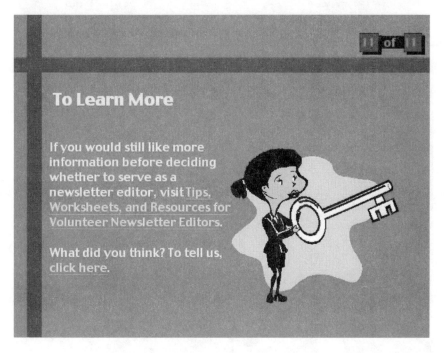

want. In most cases, that does not involve reworking the content objectives. Rather, it involves making that structure visible and accessible to learners.

Information architect Richard Saul Wurman (1989) suggests five general schemes for structuring content. He calls them hat racks. They are

- category (such as Top 40, hard rock, rap, or classical music)
- time (either a real chronological order, as in an account of an event, or an implied order, such as a procedure)
- location (in reference to a place or a thing)
- alphabet (as in a telephone directory, dictionary, or encyclopedia)
- continuum (such as least to most, worst to first, and extreme conservative to extreme liberal).

For example, consider the course menu shown in figure 6-3, which lists content in a time sequence.

Consider the Names of Segments. E-learning programs use different terminology schemes to name the individual parts (segments). Table 6-1 provides some of the most common naming schemes. In e-learning, you will hear all these terms used because no industry standard exists. Define the terms as you use them and make sure others are aware of your definitions and usage.

Figure 6-3. A course menu that uses a continuum "hat rack."

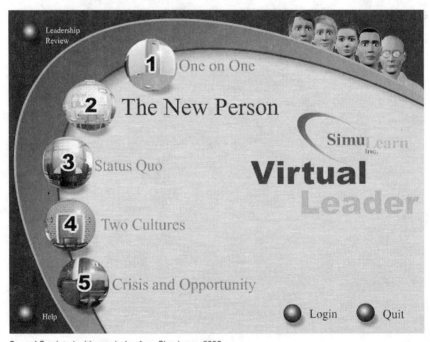

Source: Reprinted with permission from SimuLearn. 2002.

Table 6-1. Some common terminology used for naming segments of e-learning programs.

Entire Learning Program	Learning program Course Lesson Tutorial Communication product Learning product
Segment	Module Lesson
Section Within a Segment	Topic Section

Create Small Packages of Content. Attention spans for online content are unbelievably short; informal surveys of e-learning designers indicate that online learners have between five and 15 minutes' worth of attention for asynchronous lessons and between 15 and 30 minutes' worth of attention for synchronous ones. Of course, these figures vary among individuals based on their motivation for learning the course content and the extent to which that material engages the learner, but they do provide some time guidelines. In other words, it is unrealistic to expect someone to sit through a four-day course online, even if that's how long it lasted in the classroom.

In some cases, the short attention span results from the medium. Although people spend hours in front of a computer screen, they multitask (that is, perform several activities at once), surf (that is, they frequently move among screens and Websites), and are easily distracted (by telephone calls, incoming email, and similar distractions).

In some cases, the short attention span results from the motivation behind the learning. In others, learners want to learn a well-defined skill. As soon as they do so, learners consider themselves to be finished, even if the online learning program has much more material left.

You need not respond to these short attention spans by eliminating content. Rather, respond by chunking online learning programs into short, five- to 20-minute segments, much as a soap opera writer chunks a six-month-long story into daily segments. For example, consider the example of a newsletter shown in figure 6-4. It condenses a learning point to a brief article, then refers learners who want to learn more to a thorough discussion.

In practical terms, chunking content into small lessons means that you address only one main objective per segment. In the case of an extremely complex online learning program, you may only cover one supporting objective in a segment. If one segment builds on another, you can design the program so learners take segments in sequence.

Figure 6-4. Excerpt from a weekly email newsletter offering tips for designing and managing e-learning projects.

Source: "Online Learning E-News." Reprinted with permission from VNU Business Media (www.vnulearning.com). 2001.

If the segments do not relate to one another, you can design the program so learners can take segments in any order.

For planning purposes, you can estimate the length of a segment by the number of screens. Assuming your screens are fixed size (that is, the size of the screen is the same size of the monitor and does not require scrolling), a rule of thumb for estimating is one screen per minute. After developing the online learning program, verify its estimated time by timing learners.

Plan for Remediation, Enrichment, and Alternative Paths. Some learners do not grasp the material on the first try, other learners apply the material in a unique way, and still others will want to learn more about the topic. The best way to address these diverse needs is by designing with these learners in mind after you have devised the general structure for the entire learning program.

Identify material that learners might have difficulty grasping. Next, identify points where the learners' difficulties become apparent. This point is usually reached after a quiz or exercise, in which learners have an opportunity to demonstrate their proficiency. At this point, plan for remediation—that is, ongoing review of the content until learners master it. Some instructional designers have learners go through again the material presented earlier.

Because learners did not grasp the material the first time, they are less likely to grasp it the second time. A more appropriate strategy is using an alternative presentation of the content. It should also make use of other approaches, such as visual ones (if the previous presentation primarily relied on text). Also, begin the assessment with simpler practice questions.

In some instances, a significant minority of the learners will use the content in a particular environment. For example, 30 percent of the learners in a business writing class might work in a customer service center. In such situations, you can help them make more effective use of the learning material by describing its application to the learners' environments. For example, you might add a paragraph or two to the learning content that says "application in customer service" or provide specialized exercises and test questions for customer service center staff.

After completing a section, some students will want to learn more about the content. In some cases, enrichment may involve exercises that go above and beyond the presented content, or it may involve a listing of resources where learners can continue their learning.

Represent the Structure with an Information Map. After devising the structure for the learning program, record it. Although most people are trained to use outlines to represent the structure of a learning program, consider using information maps instead. As its name suggests, an information map is a diagram that shows the overall structure of a learning program, and it makes the program more visible and easier to follow.

Generally, an information map has major nodes and minor nodes. Major nodes represent major sections of a learning program; minor nodes represent subsections. See figure 6-5 for an example.

Figure 6-5. An example of an information map.

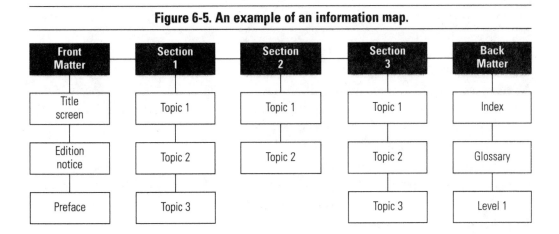

The Next Step: Pick Your Presentation Strategy

After you have chosen a format and structure for the online learning program, your next design challenge is conceiving a strategy for presenting the content. In some instances, you develop a general strategy for presenting all of the material in the online learning program. In other instances you develop different strategies for different sections and subsections because the content is sufficiently different among them that the same presentation strategy will not work in all the sections. The sections below explore the most common types of presentation strategies used in online learning programs. See the companion Website (http://saulcarliner.home.att.net/oll/index.html) for links to examples of programs that use these strategies.

Classical Approach. In a lesson designed according to the classical approach, the instructor transmits information to learners through an online presentation, or lecture. The lecture can be an extended reading passage, an online video, or an audio clip. In some cases, videotaped and audiotaped lectures are also transcribed so learners can follow along as the instructor speaks. Learners then discuss the lecture points either through a synchronous discussion with online chats or collaboration software, asynchronously through message boards or listservs, or in study groups (which might meet synchronously online, asynchronously online, or in person).

The typical structure of a classical lesson consists of seven steps:

1. Gain learners' attention.
2. Present an overview of the content.
3. Present the learning material (this would be the lecture or reading material).
4. Discuss the learning material online (either synchronously or asynchronously).
5. Provide practice problems.
6. Summarize the content.
7. Test learners.

The classical approach is popular for academic courses. It is also popular for some soft-skills courses, especially those involving interaction with others, such as leadership and advanced management. The classical approach is also popular for advanced technical subjects.

Mastery Learning. In a lesson designed for mastery learning, the lesson begins with an explanation of a psychomotor or cognitive skill. The skill is explained to learners, then demonstrated for them. Next, learners practice the skill and continue doing so until they master it (hence, the name mastery learning).

Mastery learning is popular for teaching technical skills to novices, especially when learners must perform those skills in a prescribed manner. For example, the mastery model is an ideal approach to teaching basic installation and troubleshooting procedures, as well as introductory word processing. The mastery model is also useful for teaching other types of skills, especially ones like time management that require little or no interaction with other people.

Typically, a lesson designed according to the mastery model follows this structure, which corresponds to Gagne's (1985) events of instruction:

1. Gain learners' attention.
2. Present an overview of the content.
3. Explain the material.
4. Demonstrate the skill.
5. Let learners practice the skill with close supervision, providing positive or negative feedback at each juncture.
6. Let learners continue practicing the skill, reducing the amount of feedback until they can perform the skill without assistance. For example, learners might only receive feedback if they make an incorrect choice.
7. Summarize the content.
8. Test learners.

Because experienced learners do not need this level of supervision, some designers take an abridged form of the mastery approach when designing technical training. This modified approach proves especially useful when users who have extensive experience with related content need merely to adapt or transfer their knowledge. For example, you might use modified mastery approach to the training associated with a new version of a software application. Users of the earlier version already know how to use the software; they just need to learn what's changed and how to use the new functions and features. In such instances, the lesson follows this structure:

1. Briefly introduce the topic.
2. Let learners try the skill on their own, and only provide feedback when learners make incorrect choices.
3. For learners who demonstrate mastery on the first try, provide a brief summary and, if needed, a test.

For learners who do not demonstrate mastery, take them through a full mastery lesson or provide extensive feedback on the errors, then let them try again.

Discovery Learning. In a lesson designed for discovery learning, learners first encounter a problem that figuratively or literally places them in a real-world situation. By responding to the problem, learners "discover" the key learning points (hence, the name discovery learning). A debriefing that follows can elicit and reinforce those learning points. The initial problem and the resultant discovery learning can take many forms, such as a simulation or case study.

A discovery learning experience typically follows this structure:

1. A brief introduction presents the main objective of the lesson.
2. The problem can take the form of a simulation, a case study, or another type of exercise. The main challenge in choosing a problem is finding one that richly represents the content to be addressed in the lesson yet remains simple enough that a novice can address it. The problem should be a learning experience, not a trick question.
3. The debriefing of the problem typically begins with a discussion of tangible experiences stemming from the learning. Next, it explores learners' feelings about the activity and the learning experience. Last, it abstracts the key learning points from the exercise, ideally accomplished through an interactive discussion.
4. Reinforcing the learning points by presenting them in more detail with additional support. For example, through a simulation exercise, management students may have identified key issues to consider when giving a performance appraisal. The reinforcement may suggest specific practices to follow and present data from research studies.
5. If needed, offer a second learning problem to give learners an opportunity to practice the skills.
6. Summarize the key learning points.
7. Test learners.

Discovery learning is popular for teaching skills in which learners must make judgments. For example, the discovery model is useful for teaching management skills, where decision making is integral to the job. It is also useful for teaching advanced troubleshooting and customizing skills, especially for people who will troubleshoot problems or customize software and other high-tech products in ways that the existing documentation does not address.

Blended Learning Approach. As its name suggests, a blended e-learning program combines several approaches. Typically, part of a blended learning program is presented online, and part is presented in a classroom. Of the online components, parts are designed for formal learning and other parts are designed for informal learning. Mantyla (2001) suggests that blended courses are typically designed like sandwiches: that is, two parts in one format, separated by one piece in another (figure 6-6).

Figure 6-6. Blended learning "sandwiches."

For example, one of the best-known examples of blended courses is IBM's management training. The training begins online with the background material. Learners work in groups online, using online collaboration tools to discuss the learning material and complete the assignments. The training continues with a classroom segment, which is characterized by extensive discussion. Additional online resources continue the learning process after the classroom session.

When designing blended courses, instructional designers typically place the following types of material online:

- prerequisite skills, especially ones that a large percentage of learners already possess
- rote-learning material
- reading material, such as textbooks, cases, and reference material
- study problems.

In contrast, instructional designers typically plan for the practice of interpersonal skills and discussions of higher-order thinking skills in the classroom. In a blended scenario, training truly becomes a *process* of learning rather than a learning *event.*

Learning Without Instruction. As mentioned in chapter 1, much online learning is informal; that is, the learner identifies the outcomes. In such instances, learners often seek only the content. Time-pressed learners just want the facts; they'll figure out how to apply them. Learners with extensive subject matter expertise are primarily interested in verifying their knowledge. Other learners are looking for a high-level overview of the content. If the overview suggests that they can make more extensive use of the content, learners will enroll in formal learning.

In cases like these, the learning materials resemble other types of online content, including help systems, references, Webzines, and wizards. In most instances, the format that you choose dictates the strategy for presenting the content.

If you are only designing and developing one such learning program, then you have a presentation strategy already. If you are designing and developing several related noninstructional learning programs, then your presentation strategy should focus on linking those pieces together: suggesting when learners would choose one program over the others and guiding learners to the appropriate program.

Typically, instructional designers create a home (or portal) page that categorizes the content available and provides links to it. If you want to encourage learners to visit this site often, design the home or portal page so that the content constantly changes. The new content provides learners with an incentive to visit.

The online learning program should also include a roadmap to provide learners with a path through the various pieces of content, much like the "ASTD Roadmap to E-Learning" (http://www.astd.org/virtual_community/Comm_elrng_rdmap/roadmap .html).

YOUR TURN

In this chapter you learned how to develop a high-level plan for your e-learning. You also learned about the key characteristics of adult learners and why it is important to incorporate these characteristics in your design plan. The chapter also gave you some pointers on structuring content and how to plan for all eventualities in your course, including remediation for learners who did not get the content the first time. Finally, you learned about the five most common approaches to presenting content and how to use these in your approach to e-learning.

Use worksheet 6-1 to record your design decisions to get started on your own e-learning project. If you follow the advice given in this chapter, you should have a good high-level strategy formed to help you get down to details in the next chapter.

Worksheet 6-1. Create a high-level design for your e-learning course.

1. Organize the content for your learning program, including both the course elements and sequencing the objectives. Use the following chart to help you.

Course Front Matter	Title screen Main menu Edition notice Preface Instructions on how to take the course	
Unit One	Front matter	Introductory screen Menu of topics
	Objectives to be covered	Organize the content in the objectives: • Category • Time • Location • Alphabet • Continuum
	Back matter	Descriptive summary Assessment of learning Resources

Unit Two	Front matter	Introductory screen Menu of topics
	Objectives to be covered	Organize of the content in the objectives: • Category • Time • Location • Alphabet • Continuum
	Back matter	Descriptive summary Assessment of learning Resources
Unit Three	Front matter	Introductory screen Menu of topics
	Objectives to be covered	Organize the content in the objectives: • Category • Time • Location • Alphabet • Continuum
	Back matter	Descriptive summary Assessment of learning Resources
Additional Units	Repeat the same approach that you did for the previous units	
Course Back Matter	Course exam Index Glossary Satisfaction form	

2. Determine the overall instructional strategy for presenting the content in each unit or lesson in the program. When doing so, consider the type of learning objective to be taught, the dominant learning style among learners, the attention span of the learners, and what you feel most comfortable producing.

Choose among the following approaches:
- classical
- mastery
- discovery
- blended
- learning without instruction

7

Designing the Content, Part 2:
Getting Down to Details

Now that you have completed your high-level design, you can create the detailed design for your online learning program. This chapter explains how to prepare one. Specifically, it explains how to first develop a prototype (or sample) section. This chapter explains how to plan the presentation of specific content, develop screen designs, test the proposed design, and address issues arising in the test. Next, this chapter develops storyboards for each additional screen in the learning program. In chapter 8, you will learn how to complete the designs by establishing guidelines and templates, and developing the project schedule, budget, and staffing plan.

PREPARE A PROTOTYPE SECTION

If this e-learning project is your first one, or if it is the first one for a particular group, you need feedback on all aspects of its design as you prepare the program. However, the practical reality is that sponsors and learners have a difficult time giving useful feedback on project plans. They have an easier time commenting on a finished product.

To avoid a *Catch 22* situation—needing finished designs to get feedback but not getting useful feedback without finished designs—some designers suggest developing a sample section—a prototype—to present the look and feel of the online learning program (figure 7-1). After seeing the prototype, sponsors and prospective learners can provide feedback on the general tone and approach, screen design, the ease of finding information (called navigation), and similar issues.

You must decide which type of prototype to create:

- A fully working prototype, which is a completely developed and programmed lesson, includes audio and video sequences. The sequences are only prepared in sample form, to avoid the high expenses of production. (You might shoot them with the built-in camera on the system, rather than a high-quality digital camera.)

Figure 7-1. Example of a prototype screen prepared with Microsoft PowerPoint.

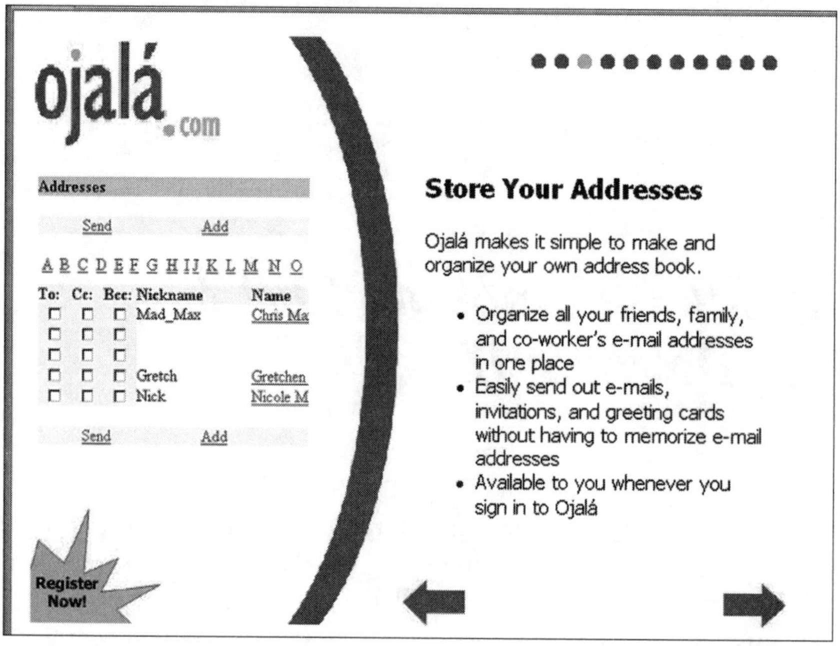

Source: Reprinted with permission of Ojalá. Prepared by Cesira Daukantas and Bethany Bishop. 2002.

■ A paper prototype (which can be presented on a computer) looks much like the final product would, but it has not been programmed. For example, if the learning program includes a test and learners are to receive feedback as they respond to questions, the prototype would only state what would happen if the learner answered a question. It does not actually display the response.

■ A partially working prototype includes some of the details missing in a paper prototype but does not include all the parts that a fully working prototype does.

Which type of prototype should you use? The answer depends on several factors. Admittedly, the more complete the prototype, the more thorough the feedback can be. But, the more complete the prototype, the more work required to develop it. Many people choose a partially working prototype to balance the need for feedback with the workload necessary to create it.

FOUR APPROACHES TO PRESENTING CONTENT

After deciding on the type of prototype, the next challenge is a creative one: how to present the learning content. As part of the high-level design, you prepared a general approach. For example, you might have chosen to present content using the mastery model. The approach tells you the general sequence of events.

At this point, you need to determine exactly how to communicate that information. For example, if you are going to describe the five common presentation strategies for e-learning, will you do so using stories? Examples? Dictionary definitions? Pictures? Other means? A combination? If you are going to present an exercise, what will it cover?

The rest of this section provides some suggestions for presenting content. Because the suggestions for presenting content overlap with the means of developing content, you'll see some additional suggestions in chapter 9, along with more specific suggestions on how to write and present content online. (Note: The process of creating content is often called writing, but because it also involves visual communication and design of interactions, the broader term *development* is more apropos to e-learning.)

Consider the General Issue of Presenting Content

Go through the online learning program, one screen at a time, and determine what will be on the screen and how it will be presented. Specifically, you need to address these issues:

- Which objective(s) will be covered on the screen? The objectives should come directly from the list of learning objectives presented earlier. In some instances, you might need several screens to present a single learning objective. In other instances, you might cover several learning objectives on the same screen. This really depends on the material.
- How will the objectives be presented—text, graphics, audio, video, or a combination? Not only do you indicate the medium, you also indicate what will be presented in the medium. For example, if you plan to present an animation sequence, indicate what it covers.

Prepare draft versions of the graphics, audio and video clips, and the programming. You also prepare screens for the front and back matter of the sample lesson: the title screen, menu screen, summary, tests, and links to additional information.

Present Content Creatively

As you prepare the plans for presenting and reinforcing the content stated in the learning objectives, consider creative ways of doing so. Here are some ideas:

- *Tell a story:* Just as you might do in a classroom, consider telling a story. For example, if you are presenting material on closing a sale, you might present information about a particular sale (perhaps someone trying to close a sale for $150,000 worth of computer equipment). Storytelling demonstrates the practical application of otherwise abstract concepts. As a variation on storytelling, give learners a more active role in the process by having them play roles in the story. For example, learners can respond to questions about how they would handle situations, as shown in figure 7-2.

- *Demonstrate the content:* Sometimes, learners need to see the concepts in real-world action. For example, learners may benefit from a demonstration of cropping a photo before learning how to do so.

- *Provide examples:* Examples illuminate concepts, much as stories do. For example, if teaching learners how to use an extensible markup language (XML) statement, in addition to describing the code, you can also show a sample of the code. Learners typically copy these examples into their own work, changing them slightly to adjust examples to their own needs. When providing examples, provide both positive examples (correct ones) and negative ones (incorrect ones). In most instances, the negative examples are as essential as the positive ones, so learners recognize when the material does not apply or does not work.

- *Ask questions:* Because e-learning has the capability of processing input from learners, your program can ask questions and respond to the answers. That way, learners can tailor the program to their own needs. For example, the screen shown in figure 7-3 shows the results of medical tests requested by learners in a medical simulation.

Figure 7-2. Example of a screen from Home Depot's award-winning training program for in-store personnel, in which learners address customer's needs.

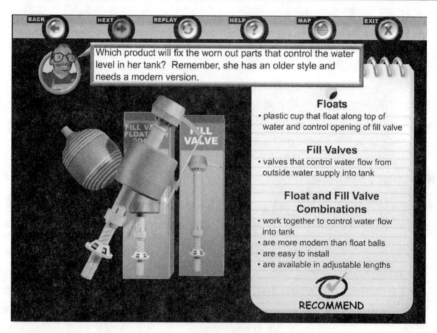

In this course, learners participate in scenarios (stories) emerging from the store environment. On this screen, an experienced sales representative coaches learners on choosing appropriate plumbing supplies.

Source: Reprinted with permission from The Home Depot. 2002.

Figure 7-3. Example of interaction within a course.

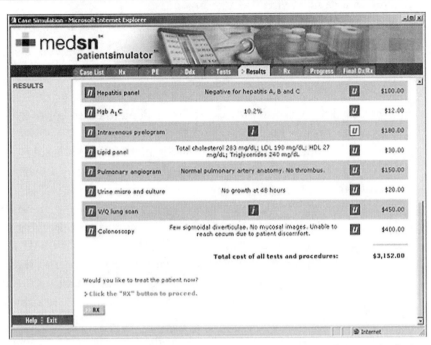

On this screen from a medical simulation, learners receive the results of medical tests they had ordered earlier. Learners click on the icons marked *n* to see what's a normal response to a given medical test. Learners click on the *i* icon to see images, such as radiographic studies. Learners click on the *u* icon to receive feedback on the utility of a medical test that they had ordered earlier in the simulation.

Source: Reprinted with permission of Medsn.com. 2001.

■ *Explain the content:* In addition to the approaches just described, also explain the content directly. For example, if the learning objectives require you to present the two dominant models of legislative government, you should name and describe them.

Use Media Other Than Text to Present Content

One of the common tendencies of e-learning developers is to use text to present content. But, because online communication is primarily an audiovisual experience (more about this in chapter 9), consider using other media to get the message across. Here are some possibilities:

■ *Visuals (illustrations or graphics):* Some content is more effectively shown rather than described. For example, numbers are easier to visualize than to read. People respond more completely to a picture of a thing rather than a verbal description of it. People follow processes by seeing their flow rather than reading a paragraph about them. Sometimes, an image like this one communicates an idea more effectively than words:

- *Photographs:* Photographs provide realistic depictions of content and show real-world environments.
- *Animation:* In some instances, the content portrayed in a visual works best when it "moves." For example, the best way to see the way a machine works is to show it working.
- *Narration:* An audio track usually involves someone speaking aloud the learning points. In some cases, the learning points are scripted. In other cases, the learning points are collected from recorded interviews with SMEs. In some online learning programs, the audio tracks are transcribed and learners have the choice of following along or turning off the audio and just reading the text. Transcribing is important for learners who have a short attention span (because learners can read three times as fast as they hear) and when the primary language of learners is a language other than that spoken by the narrator. In a few instances, the audio track consists of audio cues that learners must master, such as the sound of a particular warning and machine sounds that indicate a problem.
- *Video:* Video allows learners to see and hear the content. In some cases, video serves the same purpose as animation, but uses real-world content rather than illustrations of it. In other cases, video is used for storytelling, portraying interpersonal interaction with an immediacy that text, audio, and photographs—alone or in combination—cannot.
- *Mixed media:* A typical e-learning lesson usually consists of several media. Even the simplest program consists of text and graphics; more complex ones consist of animations and photographs, as well as audio and video sequences. Programs that use mixed media do so because each medium addresses a different educational need: text to efficiently communicate content, graphics to visually represent ideas that text cannot adequately express, audio to reinforce reading and provide cues, and video to reinforce storytelling and show interpersonal interactions. For example, consider the screen from a synchronous course shown in figure 7-4.

When choosing media, consider some of the practical issues facing your project, including the following:

- *Budget:* One of the reasons that instructional designers choose text so frequently is that it is the easiest to develop with the skills they possess. In many

Figure 7-4. Example of a screen from a synchronous course.

Your Turn to Collect the words

- **Pick a subject from either food, sports, or news.**
- **Using your browser, access one of the following sites:**
  - **http://www.foodtv.com   (Food)**
  - **http://www.espn.com   (Sports)**
  - **http://www.cnn.com   (News)**

- **Jot down as many words that describe documents found on the site you chose**

Ve**rity**

Notice the photo of the instructor in the corner, so learners can "see" the instructor, Debbie Smigocki.

Source: Reprinted with permission of Verity Corporation. 2002.

instances, developing graphics, photographs, animations, audio, and video requires outside labor that is beyond the scope of the budget.

■ *Technical capabilities of the software:* In some organizations, restrictions on the internal technology infrastructure limit or prevent the use of audio and video. Usually, the use is limited because the networks slow down significantly when using this type of information. Similarly, some learners might connect to the network through dial-up lines, slowing the transmission of audio and video sequences. In other cases, learners' systems do not have audiovisual capabilities. In such instances, these practical issues might cause you to avoid using media other than text and graphics, even if those media would work educationally.

■ *The learning environment:* Sometimes the technology infrastructure is hospitable to all media, but the learning environment is not. For example, learners who work in cubicles, bullpens, and other shared work environments might disturb their colleagues with audio.

Reinforce Learning

One of the most powerful teaching tools is use of recurring explanations, examples, and graphics to reinforce learning. Seeing the same content in different units reinforces points for learners and allows them to more easily see relationships among content. When designing online learning programs, you can reinforce content through repetition by doing the following:

■ using the same words to explain the same concepts in different units

■ building on earlier explanations by using the same points

■ using similar graphics in each unit

■ extending an example from one lesson into other lessons.

ISSUES TO CONSIDER WHEN DESIGNING SCREENS

Because prototype sections are supposed to look as close to a finished program as possible, you prepare your screen designs as you prepare the prototype section. By setting up screen designs now, you can also test them and deal with issues that arise with actual learners in a usability test. After addressing those issues, you can code these designs as "standard" and use them for every screen in the online learning program. The major issues to consider when designing screens are discussed below.

Consider the Roles of Different Parts of the Screen

Because most computer users use either the Microsoft Internet Explorer or the Netscape browser, the first issue to consider is how to design around what already exists. A typical screen for a browser has a few standard sections (figure 7-5). Each component serves a specific purpose. Moving from top to bottom, the parts are:

■ *Title bar:* The application name (such as Microsoft Internet Explorer or Netscape Navigator) and the title of the Webpage are displayed here.

■ *Menu bar:* This tool displays the titles of the drop-down menus. The browser automatically inserts the menu names. As is consistent with Windows and Macintosh convention, "file" is always the left-most menu option, next is "edit." The right-most options are "window" (always the next-to-last option) and "help."

■ *Button bar:* When users click on icons (symbols), the system moves somewhere else on the Web (not necessarily on the Website). For example, the "back" button takes learners to the last Webpage viewed, and the "home" button takes users to the page that appeared when the browser was first opened.

■ *Address line:* This line displays the Web address, or universal resource locator (URL), of the current page shown. Users can also type a Web address in that line, and the system will display the page at that address.

■ *Cueing area:* This is the focal point of the screen. Because the first several lines are the same on every screen, users typically tune them out when looking at a new screen and look first at the cueing area. They tend to look at the center of the screen. The message in this location is the one that has the most immediate impact on the learner. When you design screens, you primarily design what appears in the cueing area.

Figure 7-5. Parts of a screen.

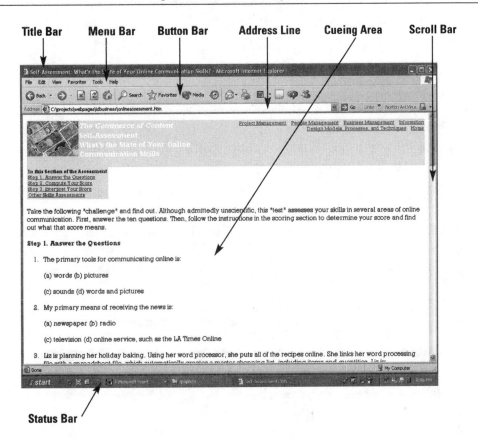

- *Horizontal and vertical scroll bars:* These tools indicate that some of the content displays off of the screen. Users must click on the bar to see the additional content.
- *The status bar:* This feature provides information about the operation of the application.

The same basic screen design applies to other types of applications running under Windows or the Mac interfaces.

Key Components of Screen Design

According to Pfeiffer (1999), page and screen design consists of these essential components:

- white space, which is blank space on the screen
- headings, which refer to section titles
- typography, which refers to the size and design of the type
- navigation, which refers to the design elements (some print, some visual) that help readers find their way through online content.

When you prepare your screen design, you work with these four components, adjusting them until you find the right look and feel for your online learning program. Figure 7-6 shows an example of a well-designed screen that effectively mixes all four elements.

Work With White Space

White space serves a number of useful purposes for readers. It frames the screen and offers the reader's eyes a rest from long blocks of text. It visually separates items, such as pictures from text, one paragraph from another, and headings from the passages that follow. Studies suggest that approximately 25 percent of the screen should be white space.

When checking your screen designs, make sure that you:

■ Leave a margin around the central block of content on the screen and any required screen elements, including the parts of the screen previously described and an optional navigation bar that you might design.

Figure 7-6. Example of a well-designed screen.

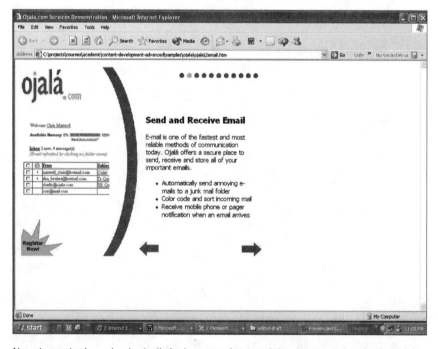

Note the emphasis on visuals, the limited amount of text, and the placement of navigational information in easy-to-find spots (the location in the tutorial is noted above, back and next buttons located in the lower right corner).

Source: Reprinted with permission from Ojala. Prepared by Bethany Bishop for Ojala. 2002.

- Leave space between blocks of content.
- Allow space between paragraphs, either indenting the first line of a paragraph or leaving a blank line between two paragraphs.
- Leave some space between a heading and the text that follows.
- Insert a blank line between an illustration or graphic and text above and below it. If you place an illustration or graphic beside a block of text, leave a two-character column of space.
- If the learning program will be translated from English to another language, leave another 25 percent of the screen blank (that is, in addition to the above). English is a compact language, so expressing the same thoughts often takes more space in other languages.

Your eye is the best judge of whether white space is needed. If a screen looks a little full with text, add white space to the area that looks crowded.

Use Consistent Headings

Headings help learners easily find content. A typical reader skims the headings to identify the importance of the various sections and identify the content covered in it. The size of the heading in relation to other headings signifies the importance of the section that follows: the larger the type size, the more significant the section.

By using a consistent system of headings, designers can signal information to learners. The system is characterized by levels of headings, much like an outline is. The lower the heading number, the larger its size and the more significant the material that follows. A typical hierarchy is depicted in table 7-1.

Use the same heading levels to identify sections at the same level in the hierarchy, and format heading levels in the same way throughout the learning program (that is, using the same typeface and size).

Table 7-1. Hierarchical system for headings.

Heading Level	Apply to This Type of Text
Level 1	Chapter heading
LEVEL 2	Major section within a chapter
Level 3	Subsection within a section
LEVEL 4	Smaller section within a subsection

Learn the Lingo of Type

Because conversations about typography extensively use terminology, you should know the basic terms of type. Table 7-2 defines some terms often used in typography.

Table 7-2. A miniglossary of typography terms.

Term	Definition
Type font	A complete set of characters in one typeface.
Typeface	A particular look or design for the set of characters. This is a serif type A. This is a san serif type H.
Point	A unit of measure for type. One point is 1/72 of an inch. Most type for reading is between 8 and 14 point. The ideal type size for reading is 11 point.
Leading (pronounced ledding)	The amount of space between lines. Generally, the leading between two lines of type is the size of the type plus 2.
Kerning	The amount of space between letters. To squeeze more type onto a line, for example, a designer would reduce the kerning. To align text on the right margin, a designer might increase the kerning to spread out the letters over the length of the line.

Be Consistent When Choosing Fonts and Type Size

What follows are some general guidelines for using type online. For more in-depth guidelines, see the companion Website for this book (http://saulcarliner.home .att.net/oll/index.html).

Generally, you should use only two fonts on the screen—one for headings, one for body text—or you should use the same font for everything. The more fonts that appear on the screen, the more difficulty learners have distinguishing the text. Make sure the size of body text is readable. For most typefaces, 11 point is an appropriate size for body text.

Furthermore, make sure that the two typefaces coordinate nicely; the typeface that you choose for headings should look good with the typeface you choose for body text. Generally, if you choose a serif font for one, choose a sans serif font for the other. For example, if you choose a sans serif font like Helvetica or Arial for headings, you might choose a serif font like Georgia, Century Schoolbook, or Bookman for the body text. Place heading text in bold.

Appropriately Justify Text

Justification refers to the alignment of text between the margins. Text may be left, right, center, or fully justified. Unjustified text has ragged edges. Fully justified text is brought flush with the left and right margins by the insertion of proportional spacing between words and letters. Most designers justify text on the left margin.

Use Emphasis Type Appropriately

Although emphasis type like bold and italic is supposed to call attention to text, publishing conventions limit the use of each to particular instances. Furthermore, the excessive use of emphasis type such as bolding, italic, color, underscoring, and all capital letters, works counter to the original intentions: Rather than calling attention to text, it draws attention away from it. Keep these rules of design in mind:

- Only use **bold** for headings, subheads, column headings on tables, and labels on illustrations.
- Only use *italic* for the names of published works and words from another language.
- Only use <u>underlining</u> and color for hyperlinks.
- Never use ALL CAP type (except for acronyms).

Plan a Clean, Simple Layout

Layout refers to the arrangement of elements on the screen. Thoughtful arrangement can simplify the task of learning online, help learners distinguish the most important content, draw attention to content that learners might otherwise overlook, and, perhaps most significantly, attract and maintain attention. The following items are suggestions for providing a clean, simple layout:

- *Limit each screen to one main point:* The key to keeping design simple is limiting the amount of information on a given screen.
- *Think about the size of the screen and scrolling issues.* Screens without scrolling usually work best for homepages of learning programs, tutorials, and demos (guided tours). Because research suggests that users do not scroll on homepages, users can miss options on a menu that do not appear when the system first displays a screen. Screens with scrolling usually work best for noninstructional content. Once learners reach a page of content with information they find useful, they are usually willing to scroll one or two times to see that material. If learners must scroll down more than one or two times to see the content, however, many choose not to do so and continue on the next screen. Furthermore, all users seem to dislike horizontal scrolling.
- *Consistently place information on the screen:* Some elements (for example, navigational tools; menu options; screen titles, frames for viewing video sequences, animations, and graphics; instructions; feedback) should appear in the same location on every screen in the online learning program. By training the eye to look for certain information in certain places, learners can immediately determine if the information is there and are less likely to miss it.

- *Design screens for skimming:* Research suggests that, rather than read online, learners tend to skim material until they encounter content of interest, and then they read more closely. Help the learner in this regard by using headings and presenting information as lists and charts. When presenting information in lists, make sure that you use the proper type of list. Use numbered lists only when learners must consider the points in the order in which they are presented. If the points can be read in a different order without changing the meaning, use bullets. Keep lists short, ideally seven or fewer items, to avoid overloading learners. (That said, lists must have at least two items; otherwise, they do not constitute a list.) If you have more than seven items, group them together and create one or more sublists (called nested lists).

- *Place the most important content at the center of the screen:* The cueing area of the screen is what learners focus on when a screen first appears. Visual material is the most eye catching on this part of the screen.

- *Use a consistent color scheme for the screen:* As part of the screen design, you also determine the color of the screen and elements on it, such as type. Because studies suggest that the readers can most easily read text when the contrast between the text and its background is sharpest, and because the sharpest contrast is black text on a white background, many online designers choose black on white as their basic color scheme. Designers generally choose a contrasting scheme for navigation bars on the screen (bars at the top and along the side, which list navigational information and links). Generally, these have a dark background (such as black, dark blue, maroon, forest green, and similarly dark colors) and light text (usually white or cream). A graphic designer can help you explore more complex color schemes.

Figure 7-7 shows an example of a screen that effectively applies all of these principles.

Design Standard Layouts for Recurring Types of Screens

Although the content on each screen in an e-learning program is unique, the type of content is not. Some screens present content as text, with graphics illustrating the main points. Some screens present video sequences, supported by bullet points or a transcript. Some screens instruct learners to answer questions and later provide feedback on the responses. Some screens introduce a unit. Others summarize it.

As you develop the prototype unit, identify the common types of screens. Use the layouts with screens presenting similar content elsewhere in the online learning program. A typical online learning program has one or more of these screens:

Figure 7-7. Another example of a well-designed screen from an e-learning advisory.

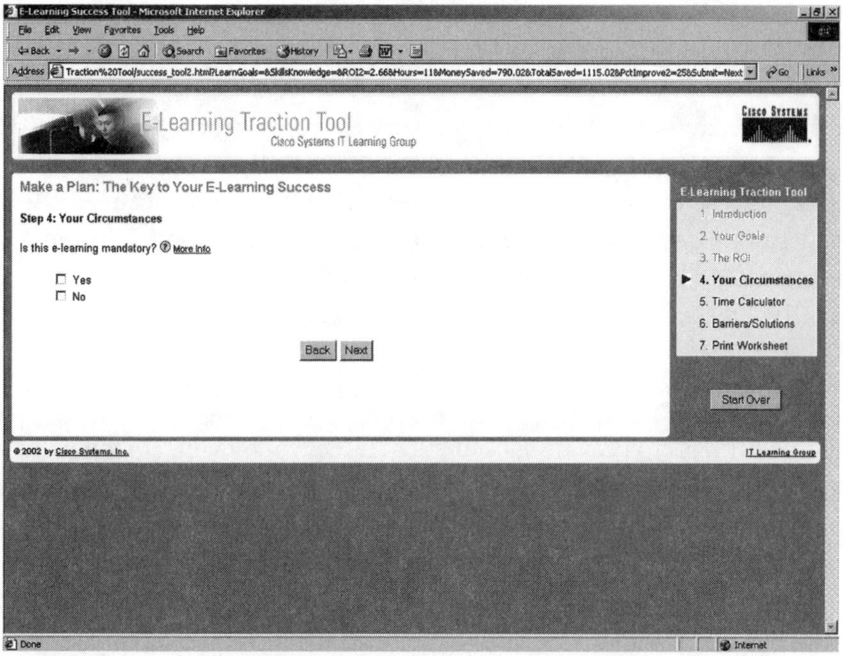

Note the short length of the screen, the generous use of white space, the limited amount of text, and the easy-to-find-and-follow instructions.

Source: Reprinted with permission of Cisco Systems. 2002.

- title screen for the unit, which is usually a graphic that presents the title of the unit and may show an information map indicating where this unit fits into the overall scheme of the learning program
- introduction to the unit, which presents a description, objectives, prerequisites, and similar material
- menu, which lists topics in the unit
- text-only screens to present content through text only
- text and graphics screens to ensure that the text and graphic appear in the same position throughout the learning program
- video screens, which usually include a frame for the video image, controls for the video player, and related materials
- audio track screens, which generally include controls for the audio player and related materials, such as visuals mentioned in the audio track, a photograph of the speaker, and bullet points or transcript of any narration that appears in the audio track
- quiz or exercise, including instructions that should not vary throughout the course

■ feedback screens to give feedback to learners and, when appropriate, uses standardized wording to give feedback

■ unit summary, often presented as a bulleted list or as a paragraph

■ screen suggesting where to find more information.

Limit the amount of linking within instructional content. Although online users find links helpful, they can also be distracting, especially if the linked-to content is not directly related to the content of the lesson. Linking also encourages learners to leave the lesson; many link out and never link back to the lesson. Therefore, consider leaving out all links in the middle of the lesson unless they are necessary, such as links to terms in the glossary. Place all links at the end of the e-learning program.

Help Learners Navigate Through the Program

Use navigational tools to provide assistance to learners in moving among parts of the e-learning program. Although browsers used with many e-learning programs provide some navigational tools, these tools often fail to meet all the needs of learners. Therefore, make sure you include the following:

■ *A title at the top of every screen indicating the name of the program, unit, and topic within the unit:* This aid helps learners determine exactly where they are working within the program. For example, to indicate to the learner that he or she is on the first of 10 screens for the topic "changing text" in the unit "editing features" in the course "Using Microsoft Word," the following would appear at the top of every screen:

Using MS Word ➦ Editing Features ➦ Changing Text (1 of 10)

■ *A link to the table of contents (main menu) of the entire learning program:* If units also have tables of contents of their own, provide a link to the table of contents for the unit the learner is currently taking—not every one in the learning program. Make sure that the two types of menus are clearly differentiated. You might call one a "course menu" and the other a "lesson menu."

■ *Instructions on how to move forward and backward:* Although most browsers provide this feature, too, the screen stored in the browser's memory is the last screen visited, which may not be the previous screen in the lesson. That's why lessons usually include separate backward and forward buttons. Furthermore, these buttons should appear at the bottom of the screen, with the forward button in the lower right corner (where one would manually touch a page to turn it) and the backward button immediately to its left (which would mimic the location learners would touch in a book to turn to the previous page).

■ *Links to a glossary and index:* Add links to these items in the back matter if they are available.

■ *Site map:* This provides a detailed (and, ideally visual) overview of the content in the learning program.

■ *Link to instructions:* Although some online learning programs call this "help," it's rarely the type of help that most learners seek when they're in trouble. You might therefore consider using a different term for this type of content.

Check for Organizational Standards

Many organizations have guidelines for screen design, especially for content that appears on the Web. Therefore, before preparing your own screen designs, find out which guidelines, if any, your organization already has and that you must follow. The most likely sources for these standards are the communications department and the information systems department. If you do have a choice, develop two or three alternative designs and test them with learners as part of the usability test of the prototype section.

DEVELOP THE PROTOTYPE

After you plan the detailed presentation and design the screens, develop all of the content for one prototype topic. As you do so, write all the text; prepare working drafts for the graphics, audio, and video (you can refine and rerecord later if need be); and, perhaps, program some of the content.

CONDUCT A USABILITY TEST OF THE PROTOTYPE

A usability test is a test of your learning product with typical target learners. As learners use the materials, independent observers record responses and make the development team aware of the issues that arose during the review. Usability tests are essential for asynchronous courses because learners must be able to use them without assistance.

Usability tests are complex and thorough. They are performed by usability engineers who plan and conduct the tests. Usability engineers provide a test plan and first conduct a trial test before conducting the actual test. At the end of the process, the usability engineer presents a report of the findings, including a list of problems and priorities for resolving them. It is your job to prepare an action plan that indicates how you will address each problem.

For more detailed instructions on conducting a usability test, see the companion Website (http://saulcarliner.home.att.net/oll/index.html).

DEVELOP STORYBOARDS

After you have developed a prototype, tested it, and responded to the issues raised in the test, it is time to plan the rest of your online learning program. Although it may seem expedient to begin developing the rest of the program at this point, it is more efficient to develop storyboards (also called wireframes) for each screen in the entire online learning program. A storyboard is a form on which you record the plans for a given screen. Figure 7-8 shows an example of a storyboard.

Storyboards document the following:

- *Learning objectives to be covered on the screen:* The objectives should come directly from your list of learning objectives. In some instances, you may need several screens to present a single learning objective. In other instances, you might cover several learning objectives on the same screen. The storyboard also indicates how the objectives will be presented—text, graphics, audio, video, or a combination. Not only do you indicate the medium, you also indicate what is to be presented in the medium. For example, if you plan to present an animation sequence, indicate what it covers.

- *Production instructions:* Describe the media used on the screen (graphics, photographs, animation, audio or video sequences). By describing the proposed content in detail, the project manager can estimate the cost of the project more accurately.

Figure 7-8. An example of a storyboard.

Screen __ of XX

APPLICATION NAME—FILE NAME   title bar
                            Window   Help
☐   ☐   button bar
                  ⬇   address line

Objective to be covered: _____

_____

How the content will be presented: _____

_____

_____

⬅   Horizontal Scroll Bar   ➡
STATUS BAR

Production instructions: _____

_____

_____

Programming instructions: _____

_____

■ *Programming instructions:* Indicate all links (include the URLs) other than standard navigation, all data processing that must be performed (such as the processing quiz answers), and any other programming needs. More specifically, you would describe the learner's input and the expected output. For simulations, indicate all the possible paths that users may take. For tutorials, indicate the correct and incorrect responses for each question, and what should happen when users choose them.

Admittedly, preparing storyboards at this level of detail for each screen involves a great deal of work, but the investment of time and effort pays off in several ways. By working through the content before you have written it, you can find redundant content and remove it. Conversely, you can spot interrelated content and strengthen the relationships through coordinated examples and planned repetition.

Because of the complexity involved in producing e-learning programs, a bit of prework now can save thousands of dollars later during the development cycle. You can reduce programming costs by finding ways to standardize programming routines and contain video and animation production costs by planning shoots efficiently and reusing footage when feasible.

FINISHING THE PLANS

After you have prepared storyboards for each screen in the online learning program, you complete the process by documenting the guidelines under which the program will be developed. These guidelines address editorial, design, and programming issues, so that similar types of information are presented in similar ways. The guidelines usually include templates, which are like fill-in-the-blank forms for standardizing the presentation of content. Chapter 8 explains how to develop guidelines for an e-learning program.

Finally, you should review the entire package with SMEs and sponsors. In some instances, the two are part of the same group. The reviews give SMEs an opportunity to verify that the content is complete and accurate. The reviews give sponsors a detailed description of your plans and an opportunity to gain formal support for the plans. When sponsors approve the plans, ask for a memo stating their approval. Chapter 10 explains how to conduct reviews.

YOUR TURN

In this chapter you learned how to build a prototype, and use some creative approaches to present your content online. You also learned that different parts of the screen have different roles to play in helping your learner navigate e-learning. The appearance of your e-learning product can affect the learning experience in significant ways. Next, you learned to conduct a usability test on the prototype to make sure that designs will be effective with the intended learners. Last, you learned that, after you have finished designs, you prepare storyboards for each screen not included in the prototype.

Now it is your turn to get down to the details of designing your e-learning content. Use worksheet 7-1 to create a storyboards for a short sequence (lesson) in an e-learning project that you are working on or expect to work on.

Worksheet 7-1. Develop a storyboard for your e-learning program.

Screen __ of XX

APPLICATION NAME—FILE NAME   title bar
                                   Window   Help
☐   ☐   button bar
                      ⤓   address line

Objective to be covered: _____

_____

_____

How the content will be presented: _____

_____

_____

_____

← Horizontal Scroll Bar   →
STATUS BAR
_____

Production instructions: _____

_____

_____

Programming instructions: _____

_____

_____

_____

Review your storyboards and evaluate your design plans according to the criteria presented in worksheet 7-2.

After making revisions, show your storyboards to an intended learner, and ask that person to go through the sequence as if he or she were taking the course. Remain silent as the learner goes through, noting the problems that the learner experiences. Determine whether the learner can achieve the objective of the short sequence.

Afterward, debrief the learner about the experience of using the lesson. Do the same with a representative of your sponsor's organization. Do you notice any difference between the learners' and sponsors' reactions? What are they? How would you resolve the differences?

Worksheet 7-2. Evaluate your screen design.

Options for Presenting Content	Did you use creative presentation techniques? ☐ Storytelling ☐ Demonstrations ☐ Positive and negative examples ☐ Questions ☐ Explanations of content Did you use a variety of media to present content? ☐ Text ☐ Visuals ☐ Photographs ☐ Audio ☐ Video Did you use repetition effectively to reinforce learning? ☐ Explanations ☐ Examples ☐ Graphics
Screen Design	Did you arrange the screen in a visually pleasing and functional way? ☐ 25 percent of the screen as white space ☐ Black text on a white background with a contrasting color for the navigation bar ☐ Left justification of all text, including headings Did you make appropriate use of fonts? ☐ No more than two fonts for text and headings ☐ Serif font for body text and sans serif for headings (or vice versa) ☐ Larger fonts for lower-level headings to distinguish among heading levels Did you use emphasis type in appropriate ways? ☐ Bold for headings ☐ Italic for titles of published works and terms from other languages ☐ Underscoring and color (together) to indicate hyperlinks

8

Publishing Guidelines: How To Ensure Quality

Although you have developed a detailed blueprint for the course, it only specifies what is to be presented and how. The blueprint does not cover many of the more technical aspects of developing content. A second series of plans addresses these issues and serves a crucial role in ensuring the quality of your online learning program. This chapter addresses these guidelines, which include the following:

- style guidelines for spelling, capitalization, punctuation, usage, terminology, and typographical arrangements
- technical standards for authoring
- technical standards for the viewing system
- template standards
- production specifications.

This chapter explains how each category of guidelines applies to the development of online learning programs and shows you how to create workable guidelines for your own online learning products.

Set Style Guidelines

Should each list item end with a period or not? Should the device above the system unit be called a monitor or a display? Should periods or dashes separate the parts of a telephone number? Should the word *email* only be used as a noun or can it be used as a verb?

The correct answer to all these questions can be whatever you want. Whatever you choose to do, you need to follow that decision consistently throughout the online learning program. So, if you end list items with periods in lesson 1, then you should end them with periods in lesson 5.

The inconsistency that results from the contradictory use of terms, instructions, numbers, and punctuation on your part can confuse learners. Issues like these are called *style,* which, according to *Webster's Third New International Dictionary,* refers to the customs followed for spelling, capitalization, punctuation, usage, terminology, and typographical arrangements. All elements of style are choices, and developers of online learning programs often follow different styles in different situations.

Because the number of choices can be overwhelming and because most business communication follows a relatively standard style, most instructional designers choose a few key sources as references on all matters of style. When a question arises, instructional designers and developers consult the appropriate source, so make sure that everyone involved in development has access to and relies upon the same references.

One of those references is a dictionary, which serves as your primary authority on spelling and usage. The choice of many editors is *Merriam-Webster's Collegiate Dictionary,* currently available as the 10th edition. The other key reference is a manual of style, which addresses most other issues you will encounter, including the following:

- punctuation
- notation of scientific formulas
- use of numbers (for example, do you write a large number as 1 million or 1,000,000)
- ways to cite other sources
- headings
- appropriate entries for the table of contents.

Table 8-1 suggests manuals of style to consider in different instances. No matter how comprehensive your dictionary and manual of style are, you will encounter terms specific to your project, field of endeavor, and organization. For example, you will have to set the standards for wording for instructions and explanations, capitalization for job and department titles, specialized uses of punctuation, and specialized notations for scientific and technical formulas. The important thing is to capture these special terms and treatments in your style guide to ensure that your products are consistent, error-free, and easy for learners to use.

Before you choose a dictionary and style guide, find out whether your sponsor already has a preference. Many corporations have a chosen style guide for use in particular situations.

Similarly, note that your organization will have unique issues of terminology and style that the chosen dictionary and style guide do not address. For these, you develop a corporate style guide. Figure 8-1 shows a sample from a corporate style guide that is available online. See the companion Website (http://saulcarliner.home.att.net /oll/index.html) for information on how to develop a corporate style guide.

Set Technical Standards for Authoring

Authoring refers to the task of entering text and graphics into the computer using hardware and software. But which computer? What type of hardware? Which software? Can the technical staff in your organization support the software you use to

Table 8-1. Examples of commonly used style manuals.

Style Guide	Type of Content
The Chicago Manual of Style, currently available as the 14th edition (1993, Chicago: University of Chicago Press)	Most technical and scientific material
Publication Manual of the American Psychological Association (APA), currently available as the fifth edition (2001, Washington, DC: American Psychological Association)	Most content in the social science disciplines, including psychology, sociology, business, and economics, for which effective communication in words and data is fundamental
The Associated Press Stylebook and Briefing on Media Law, N. Goldstein, editor (New York: Associated Press) *The New York Times Manual of Style and Usage: The Official Style Guide Used by the Writers and Editors of the World's Most Authoritative Newspaper* by A.M. Siegal & W.G. Connolly (1999, New York: Times Books)	Originally developed for use by journalists but now considered the style manuals of choice for most marketing and employee communications materials
Xerox Publishing Standards: A Manual of Style and Design by Xerox Corporation (1988, New York: Xerox Press-Watson Guptill)	Although out of print now, the now-classic Xerox manual has been the basis for myriad organizational style guides
Microsoft Style Guide	Preferred for protocol about Windows-based software

author the course? Is the material produced by your authoring software must usable with the browsers and other software used to view the program on the learners' computers?

Identifying these specifications as part of the plans for an online learning program is important. By doing so, you make it possible to re-create a system with the chosen authoring tools should anything happen to the original system. Similarly, if several people work on the development of the system, these specifications ensure that all developers work with the compatible software. Table 8-2 lists some typical technical specifications for authoring online learning.

Additionally, authoring standards identify any industry standards to which the online learning program must conform, such as the Aviation Industry Computer-Based Training Committee (AICC) and Sharable Content Object Reference Model (SCORM). Both sets of standards are established to ensure that content produced on one system and managed by a particular learning management system (LMS) can be used on other systems. If you choose authoring software and an LMS that comply with these standards, the material you develop should conform, and you should be able to exchange it with other systems (ASTD, 2001).

Figure 8-1. Example of internal publishing guidelines, also called a corporate style guide.

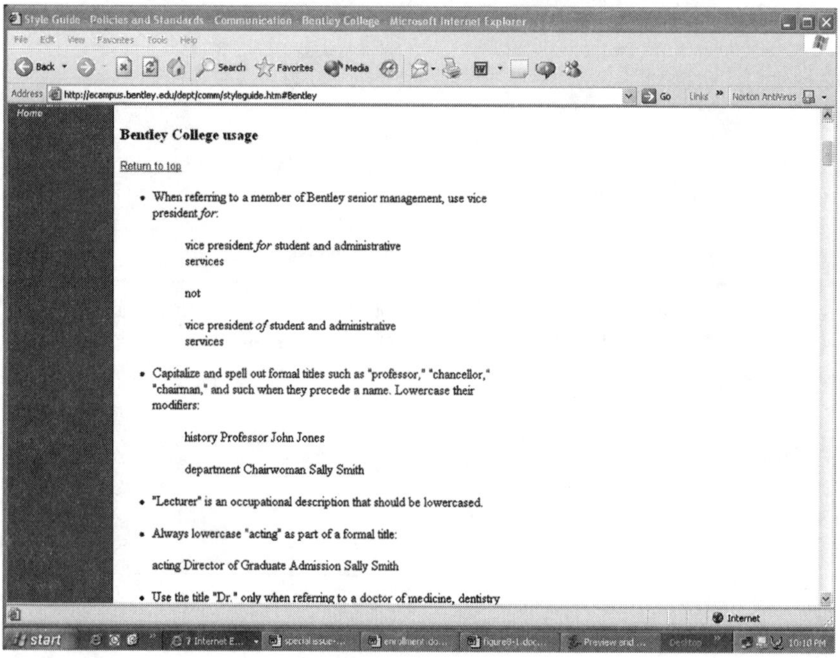

Source: Reprinted with permission from Bentley College. 2002.

SET THE MINIMUM CONFIGURATION FOR VIEWING

Viewing refers to the act of reading or taking an online learning program on a computer. However, not all learning software can be viewed on all computers. Therefore, before you actually begin to develop the program, you need to determine the minimum configuration of the computers needed to view it. Test your learning materials on computers that meet but do not exceed this minimum specification to ensure that learners using this minimum configuration will be able to complete the program without problems.

A minimum configuration for the viewing system depends on the choice of authoring software. When making the choice of authoring software, consider whether learners can realistically view it with the systems available to them.

Some of the information that you need to specify about the configuration of learners' computers is similar to that you would specify for the technical standards for authoring. Note, too, that your authoring software will also place requirements on the configuration required for viewing the online learning program. See the companion Website (http://saulcarliner.home.att.net/oll/index.html) for information about the viewing computer that you need to specify at this time.

Table 8-2. Suggested hardware and software requirements to incorporate into authoring standards.

Hardware	☐ Processor
	☐ Hard drive
	☐ Other types of storage (such as a CD, DVD, or other types of high-capacity storage drives)
	☐ Storage
	☐ Video adapter
	☐ Monitor (especially if an oversize monitor is needed)
	☐ Telecommunications capabilities (such as a network adapter or modem, and the type)
	☐ Scanner, printer, and other output devices
	☐ Digital camera
	☐ Speakers
	☐ Microphone
Software	☐ Operating system and its version (such as Windows XP, Mac OS, or Linux)
	☐ Office software (such as a word processor, spreadsheet program, or presentation graphics)
	☐ Authoring software for entering the bulk of the online learning program
	☐ Software for creating and editing graphics, clip art, and photographs
	☐ Music editing software, such as software for recording and editing content, and preparing it in an MP3 format
	☐ Educational testing software, which lets you prepare informal and formal assessments

DEVELOP TEMPLATES

A template is a special type of word processing or authoring file that you can use consistently to develop similar types of screens, thereby reducing the amount of time needed to develop an online learning program, as well as the inconsistency among lessons (because the parts that need to be consistent are often included in the template).

A template works like a fill-in-the-blank form. The content that remains consistent is entered exactly as it would appear. Blanks and instructions for filling them in are placed where developers should add information. Once the designs are firm and the editorial and authoring guidelines set, but before development begins, you develop templates to codify those guidelines.

When you develop templates, you identify the following:

■ text that is the same in every part of the online learning program
■ formatting for headings, body text, examples, figures, and other text elements; this formatting includes typography, margins, and placement of consistently

placed items, such as the text of a title or a line that might appear in the same place on every screen

■ navigation bars (if they are separately coded in each frame).

Although the technical instructions for creating templates vary among authoring tools, the procedure described in the following sections suggests how you might determine which templates to create and which information to include in them.

1. Identify Recurring Screen Types

From your design plans, identify the types of screens that occur throughout the learning program. Following are some commonly recurring screens:

■ title screens for a lessons and modules
■ menus
■ overview screens for lessons and modules
■ screens in which you present information
■ screens in which you present audio or video sequences (including the controls)
■ summaries
■ quizzes and tests.

2. Identify Common Elements on the Screen

For each type of common screen that you identify, identify all the common elements on the screen. Determine whether they will be identical on each screen or just handled in similar ways. Specifically, consider these elements:

■ headings, including the placement and wording of those headings
■ text, including text that consistently appears on each of these types of screens and the placement of that text
■ graphical elements, including boxes and other devices that appear in the same place on every instance of this type of screen.

3. Consider Typography

Determine the type font, emphasis, and size for headings, paragraphs (body text), examples, and other types of text. Of equal importance is the amount of white space on the screen. Text that is too dense is difficult to read, especially on a monitor. Take this into account as you set margins and line spacing.

ESTABLISH PRODUCTION SPECIFICATIONS

If you plan on packaging your learning product, a number of production issues must be addressed: whether to use a cardboard sleeve or a plastic CD case (jewel box), what type of paper and cover to use for printed materials, and so forth. You must also determine production specifications for any printed materials that accompany the online learning program. Table 8-3 covers most of these issues.

Table 8-3. Production specifications for your e-learning project.

Type of Communication Product	Issues to Specify
Printed materials that accompany the online learning program	☐ Paper dimensions ☐ Paper weight for cover and inside pages: Refers to the strength of the paper. The heavier the weight, the stronger the paper. For paperback books, the typical cover is cardboard stock paper, about 100 pounds. The weight of paper for a typical learning workbook is 40 or 50 pounds. ☐ Paper type for cover and inside pages: Refers to the finish of the paper. A matte paper has a dull finish but holds ink better. A glossy paper has a shiny finish and shows off photographs and other illustrations better. You might also indicate whether you want to use recycled paper. ☐ Number of print colors (if using any in addition to black). Adding a second or third color ink to the page can enhance the appearance of a communication product but also adds to the expense. If you plan to use color photographs, you will need to use four-color printing (the printing process that allows the reproduction of color photographs). ☐ Binding: Indicate whether you want the manual to be: — Shrink wrapped (wrapped in plastic) — Perfect bound (the cover wraps all around the front, back, and spine of the guide and the pages are glued to the cover) — Saddle-stitched (stapled) — Drilled with three holes so learners can insert in a three-ring (or similar) binder. ☐ Anticipated number of pages: The number of pages affects the choice of printing presses. Printers use one type of press for jobs with few pages and a web press for jobs with many pages. The number of pages also limits your binding options. For example, printers cannot use perfect binding if the guide exceeds a certain number of pages. ☐ Anticipated number of copies: Because the most expensive part of printing is in setting up the presses, printers usually offer price breaks for larger print quantities. The printer can spread the cost of setting up the presses over more copies. The more you print, then, the lower the cost per copy. If you are designing a course to be viewed on a personal digital assistant (PDA), you may also have additional viewing requirements.
CD or DVD	☐ Type of packaging: Options include a jewel box (a hard plastic case with tabs to hold a small booklet in front and space on the back to accommodate a label or a sleeve (a printed cardboard envelope in which the CD or DVD is inserted). Another option is to use a binder for the printed materials with a pocket in front to hold a CD or DVD. ☐ Number of colors for booklet and label ☐ Quantity to be reproduced ☐ Printing on the CD or DVD (if any)

USING GUIDELINES

Guidelines are only useful if developers follow them. Templates simplify the effort of conforming to guidelines because many of the issues are already addressed in the template.

During reviews that occur later in the development process, others will check to make sure that the guidelines are being followed. Editorial reviews provide an opportunity to make sure that materials conform to style guidelines. Tests provide an opportunity to make sure that materials conform to authoring and viewing standards. See chapter 10 for an in-depth discussion of reviews.

YOUR TURN

Take some time now to set up your own quality guidelines using worksheet 8-1.

Worksheet 8-1. Set your own publishing quality measures.

1. Choose a style manual based on the type of content you are developing.

Scientific and Technical (Post-sales) Employee Communications
- ☐ Chicago style
- ☐ Other:_____

Scientific and Technical (Pre-sales) Employee Communications
- ☐ Associated Press style
- ☐ New York Times style
- ☐ Other:_____

Social Science Communications
- ☐ APA
- ☐ Other:_____

Corporate Style Guide

Project Style Guide

2. Choose a dictionary.

- ☐ Prescriptive (such as *American Heritage Dictionary*)
- ☐ Descriptive (such as *Merriam-Webster's Collegiate Dictionary.*)
- ☐ Corporate glossary or dictionary
- ☐ Project glossary or dictionary to list exceptions and special meanings not covered in the primary dictionary

3. Develop technical standards for authoring.

Hardware Platform

☐ Processor: _____

☐ Memory: _____

☐ Hard drive: _____

☐ Graphics adapter: _____

☐ Monitor: _____

☐ ZIP drive: _____

☐ CD or DVD drive: _____

☐ Telecommunications: _____

☐ Scanner: _____

☐ Printer: _____

☐ Digital camera: _____

☐ Speakers: _____

Software

☐ Operating system: _____

☐ Office software: _____

☐ Authoring system: _____

☐ Graphics software: _____

☐ Photography software: _____

☐ Testing software: _____

☐ Music software: _____

☐ Video software: _____

☐ Browser: _____

☐ Standards to meet (such as SCORM): _____

☐ Other: _____

4. Determine the minimum configuration for viewing.

Hardware Platform

☐ Processor: _____

☐ Hard drive: _____

☐ Storage device needed: _____

☐ Storage capacity: _____

☐ Video adapter: _____

☐ Monitor: _____

☐ Telecommunications capabilities: _____

☐ Speakers: _____

☐ Microphone: _____

(continued on next page)

Worksheet 8-1. Set your own publishing quality measures (continued).

Software

- ☐ Operating system and version: _____
- ☐ Viewing software: _____
- ☐ Browser: _____
- ☐ Audio software: _____
- ☐ Video software: _____
- ☐ Other software: _____
- ☐ Browsers and versions: _____
- ☐ Plug-in software: _____

5. **Prepare templates.**

- ☐ Menus
- ☐ Overview screens for lessons and modules
- ☐ Screens in which you present information
- ☐ Screens in which you present audio or video sequences
- ☐ Summaries
- ☐ Quizzes and tests

6. **Set production guidelines.**

Type of Communication Product	Issues to Specify
Printed materials that accompany the online learning program	☐ Size of the page: _____ ☐ Weight and type of paper for the cover: _____ ☐ Weight and type of paper for inside pages: _____ ☐ Number of colors: _____ ☐ Shrink wrapped ☐ Perfect bound ☐ Saddle-stitched ☐ Drilled ☐ Anticipated number of pages: _____ ☐ Anticipated number of copies: _____
CD or DVD	☐ Jewel box ☐ Sleeve ☐ Number of colors: _____ ☐ Quantity: _____ ☐ Printing on the CD or DVD (if any): _____

9

Communicating Effectively Online

Despite much-publicized efforts to move books online and create e-books, the computer screen is an inherently different medium than the page; communicating online is inherently different than communicating in print. Communicating online has four components: communicating interactively (that is, writing a dialogue), communicating visually (that is, seamlessly integrating pictures into the message), writing through a dialogue-like grammar, and, most significantly, recognizing the unique characteristics of communicating online.

By exploring these four topics, this chapter suggests ways to effectively develop the online learning program that has been so carefully designed. Before doing so, it discusses the challenge of communicating within the framework of the design plans. The chapter closes with suggestions on how to address changes in design plans that typically arise during development.

COMMUNICATING WITHIN THE FRAMEWORK OF DESIGN PLANS

In the earlier parts of the instructional design process, you developed a detailed blueprint for the course that indicates, screen by screen, which content will be presented and how.

In some ways, this blueprint represents more than a plan. It represents a set of expectations. The sponsors of the online learning program and other members of the development team expect you to develop the program course according to these plans. Changes are feasible; indeed, sometimes they are unavoidable, but you cannot arbitrarily make them. The last section in this chapter explains the delicate process of changing plans.

You can show your creativity through the presentation of content, writing it expressly for the screen. When you develop the content, you develop it in stages. You develop a first draft, then have it reviewed by SMEs (called a technical review) and editors (called an editorial review). Using the feedback as a guide, you revise the course and prepare a second draft.

After the second draft is complete, it is reviewed again by SMEs and editors, and also undergoes tests. Some of the tests are technical tests, others are tests with prospective learners (usability tests).

Rather than concentrating on this write-and-revise process, the chapters on development concentrate, instead, on other aspects of this effort. This chapter concentrates on techniques for writing for the screen, the aspect of developing online content that is most challenging to many online course developers. Chapter 10 explains how to elicit effective reviews and how to prepare a draft for production.

THE UNIQUE CHARACTERISTICS OF COMMUNICATING ONLINE

Communicating online significantly differs from communicating on the page. One difference is the reading experience. Studies suggest that reading online is slower and of poorer quality than reading on the page. For example, after reading the first sentence or two on a screen, readers typically scan the rest of the topic or move onto the next screen. Studies also suggest that reading speeds online are slower than those on the page. The typical reader only reads 75 percent as quickly online as on the page.

Another difference is that online communication offers many possibilities that are not available on the page. The online communication experience is

- *Image oriented:* The computer display is essentially a television screen. Usually you can turn off the sound for your favorite show and still get the gist of the story. E-learning also offers powerful visual cues, although many e-learning designs still communicate through words.
- *Interactive:* The communication between a computer and a learner is a dialogue. The computer poses a question, and the learner answers. When the computer responds, the response indicates that the computer took the learner's answer into account.
- *Immediate:* Immediate has two meanings. (1) When learners make a request, they expect a response within seconds. (2) Learners expect a response based on the most current content.
- *Intimate:* Because it can store information about learners and track their progress, the computer can "know" learners, continue to learn about them, and, as a result, adapt content to learners' known interests.

Because of the differences between traditional learning and e-learning, developers of online learning programs do more than write. They use images to communicate when they might have used words on the page or in the classroom. Developers foster interaction with learners, writing text that resembles a dialogue that requires responses from learners.

Four Tips for Communicating Visually

One of the primary reasons for using visual images in online learning programs is that images hold the primary responsibility for communicating information online. Images are easier to understand than text and are remembered longer than text.

Many people assume that they must be able to draw to communicate visually. Not true. Rather, they need to be able to choose the right type of image or visual communication tool. Some tips for communicating visually are discussed below.

Visually Represent Numeric Data

Although text can convey specific numbers, it cannot convey how numbers relate to one another as efficiently, quickly, or easily as visuals can. Primarily used to show financial results and other business data, visuals in sophisticated forecasting software can help learners visualize the impact of choosing different alternatives. For example, use a pie chart to show the relationship of parts to a whole. Or, to show relationships among data over a period of time, use a histogram or bar chart or another graphic that shows data in this way. See the companion Website (http://saulcarliner.home.att .net/oll/index.html) for examples of these types of charts.

Visually Represent Concepts

The term *concepts* refers to nonnumeric data. Some concepts are concrete, such as machines, furniture, and geography. Some concepts are abstract, such as processes and symbols. Here are some ways that you might represent concepts visually:

- what things look like or where they are located: for example, the power switch on a computer
- how things work: for example, an animated sequence of turning a computer on
- procedures: for example, a flow chart showing how to program a computer, how to operate a fax machine, or how a bill in Congress becomes a law
- relationships: for example, an organizational chart
- symbols: for example, an international "no smoking" sign.

Figures 9-1 and 9-2 visually represent concepts. Figure 9-1 is a photograph of a "character" in a simulation. Figure 9-2 is a line drawing that illustrates medical concepts.

Call Attention to Text

In addition to communicating ideas visually, you can also use visual devices to call attention to specific passages of text. These visual devices can help build learners' interest in the content, differentiate must-know from nice-to-know material, and

Figure 9-1. Example of a photograph used in a course.

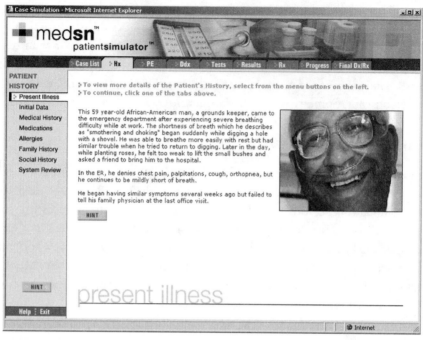

In this case, the photograph shows a "patient" whose case is used in a medical simulation and makes the simulation more realistic,

Source: Reprinted with permission from Medsn.com. 2002.

help learners easily find specific content. To draw attention to a specific passage, use one of the following:

- a box, either shaded or bordered
- a pull quote, in which you pull one of the most provocative quotes in the passage and place it in a box nearby and in a much larger type font
- a sidebar, in which amplifying text is placed in a box near the main text
- circles and arrows directing readers to specific passages.

Also, to help readers scan content rapidly, place it in charts and lists. See the companion Website (http://saulcarliner.home.att.net/oll/index.html) for examples of these approaches.

Use Visuals Effectively

Although visuals can effectively communicate ideas, keep certain issues in mind as you develop visuals to ensure that yours are as effective as possible.

Figure 9-2. Example of a line drawing used in a course.

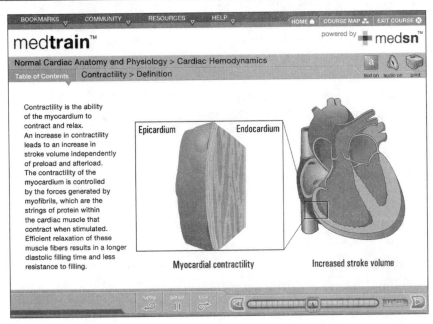

This is a medical illustration. Note the use of shading to enhance the appearance of the drawing without adding extraneous detail.

Source: Reprinted with permission from Medsn.com. 2002.

■ Use visuals for practical purposes, not adornment. Each visual should support the learning process by showing something relevant to the content. Otherwise, visuals distract learners and complicate the learning process.

■ Remove extraneous details from photographs and illustrations. Unnecessary detail is called clutter, because it clutters up the image and makes it difficult for the learner to discern the purpose of the visual. The process of removing excess information from photographs is called cropping.

■ Because they typically have less detail than photographs, line drawings have been shown to be more effective than photographs to teach technical information, such as installation and servicing of equipment. These studies also show that the irrelevant detail in photographs is distracting to learners. Figure 9-2 is an example of a line drawing used to communicate medical information.

■ Place the visual immediately after its reference in text. Try to avoid showing the graphic in a pop-up screen unless necessary. Separated from the text, learners forget the purpose of the image.

■ Label all illustrations and relevant details. Although a picture is worth a thousand words, a few words of explanation ensures clear comprehension of it.

Typical information to accompany an illustration includes a caption (as much as two sentences that appear beneath the visual and explain its purpose), the parts of a diagram (the rooms on a floor plan, the steps in a flowchart, or the parts of a product), and, for graphs, axis labels and units of measure for each axis (for example, the X axis may represent time in years and the Y axis may represent spending in millions of dollars).

■ Use stock images (clip art) carefully. Find out if your organization already has the image you are seeking. Stock images are available immediately on CDs and on the Web. Any search engine will find sources for images.

■ Even if you paid for it, do not assume that you have blanket permission to use graphics and photos from clip art libraries, photo CDs, and other departments in your organization. Most art comes with copyright restrictions and is not free, even that found on the Web.

■ Keep the size of graphic files (the ones in which visuals are stored, because visuals are stored separately from text) as small as possible. Online learners expect information to appear on the screen immediately. Large files defeat this purpose. Avoid this by using graphics with as little detail as possible.

■ Use JPEG format for photographs; files with a .jpg extension transfer more quickly than other formats do.

■ If the graphic takes a while to load, insert material that informs the learner of that fact.

Tips for Communicating Interactively

The second challenge of communicating online is that of communicating interactively. Online communication is ultimately an exchange between a learner and the computer—an interaction. Because most course developers are skilled at broadcast communication (that is, one-way communication to an audience), the experience of writing a two-part conversation is a unique one. In some cases, you are able to prepare all of the interaction on your own. In other instances, you design the interaction and a programmer assists you in realizing the design plans. It's your responsibility as a course developer to realize the opportunities for interaction as you prepare the content.

The tips offered in the following sections suggest situations where interaction is most useful.

Consider What Interaction Is (and Is Not)

Interaction refers to opportunities for learners to provide information to the system and have it respond with appropriate feedback. The most common example of interaction in an online learning program is the question. The system presents learners with a question; learners respond and receive feedback (figure 9-3). The questions can be used as a checkpoint within a section, or as a quiz or test at the end of the learning material. Most

Figure 9-3. An example of clear, simple instructions for an e-learning advisor.

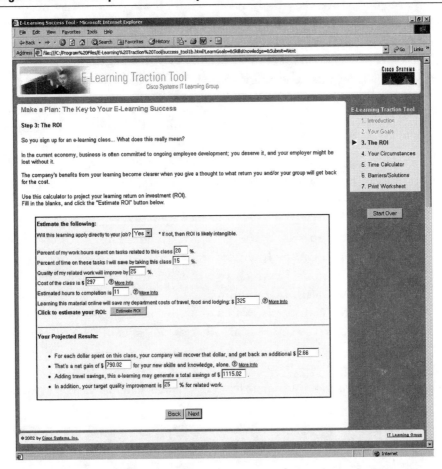

Note the clarity and simplicity of the instructions on this e-learning advisor. For example, learners would easily know that they should click on *yes* or *no* to answer the question, and *next* to continue to the next question. This clarity in screen design is called intuitive design, because learners do not require any training to use the online program.

Source: Reprinted with permission from Cisco Systems. 2002.

online learning program use forms of objective questions, such as multiple choice, matching, true/false (also yes/no), and fill-in-the-blank (usually with one or two words).

Other types of common interactions include the following:

■ drag-and-drop exercises, in which learners drag and drop something into another place, such as moving the steps of a procedure into order or the parts of a product into place

■ extended fill-in-the-blank questions, in which learners write a sentence or paragraph, rather than a single word

■ simulations to provide experiences that mimic real-world situations.

Another common type of interaction lets learners choose their own path through the course. Menus, links, and search tools are the primary means of making this happen in online learning. For example, see the choices presented to learners in figure 9-4.

Some types of interaction do not involve an exchange between the learner and the course, yet provide for interaction all the same. These include the following:

- self-assessments, which learners take before a unit or course, to identify what they already know about a subject and determine which skills they need to develop to fill in the gaps. (See "What's the State of Your Online Communication Skills?" on the companion Website for an example of a self-assessment.)
- case learning, in which learners read a case and interact with materials outside of the course, then write up their response. Although this looks like a page turner, looks deceive because the interaction occurs on a different level.
- treasure hunts, in which the online learning program directs learners to search other parts of the Internet for material, then return to the program.
- cooperative learning, in which two or more learners work together to complete the online learning program.
- bulletin boards or listservs, which allow learners to post questions and comments, and receive feedback from other participants in the program.

Figure 9-4. An example of an online learning program that lets users move around on their own.

Notice the options—different topics on plumbing products. Learners can take them in any order.

Source: Reprinted with permission from The Home Depot. 2002.

Interact Appropriately With Learners

As in the classroom, active engagement increases the attention to, and comprehension of, content in online learning programs. But, the interaction should be appropriate.

Appropriate interaction is an exchange between the learner and the online learning program that is relevant to the content. Although some interaction engages the learner, if it is not relevant to the content, it merely distracts learners and, therefore, is not appropriate. For example, suppose a course on the safe use of power tools includes a number game. Although the number game encourages direct interaction with the course, the game teaches numbers, not safety, and is not relevant. The course developer must work harder to win attention back to the safety content which, by now, might seem downright boring to learners.

Interact Frequently with Learners

The frequency of interaction in online programs varies according to which teaching model is used. Some learning models better lend themselves to interaction. The classical model of learning mainly uses tests and quizzes, so this model has the least amount of interaction, whereas the mastery model lends itself to interaction at certain key points, including the opening; demonstration; and exercises and quizzes, which usually occur at the end of a unit. The cooperative learning model elicits interaction through the process of group learning, and the discovery and experiential learning models let learners learn by doing and lend themselves to interaction through lab exercises and simulations of activities.

Provide Appropriate Feedback

When users enter material, the feedback should be appropriate to the response. For example, if learners must enter a password to get into the linked content or if they have to wait a while for the system to process the request, inform them in advance.

When responding to questions, provide immediate feedback to the response and, if appropriate, link to related content (figure 9-5). The response has three parts:

1. indication of whether the response was correct
2. explanation about why the response was not correct or some clarification on the correct content
3. instructions on how to proceed.

Here's an example of appropriate feedback: "Informal learning happens through knowledge management and performance support. Press Enter to continue."

When accepting answers, accept anticipated misspellings, unless correct spelling is a key part of the learning objective. For example, if the correct answer is "turkey" and someone responds "turky," accept the misspelling.

In some cases, when learners answer a question incorrectly, you might send them through review material. Ideally, the review sequence provides alternative explanation

Figure 9-5. Feedback to a quiz question in a medical simulation.

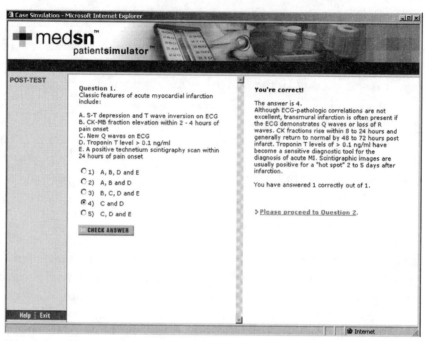

Although the subject is technical, learners who are not expert in the subject can still understand it. Notice the positive tone and the clear writing.

Source: Reprinted with permission from Medsn.com. 2002.

of the content. Had learners understood the original version of the content, they would have answered the questions correctly.

Use Controls Appropriately

In the process of interacting with users, you will most likely apply some conventions of interacting used in electronic forms, data entry, and other types of applications. Make sure that you use these conventions in ways that learners are familiar with. Table 9-1 lists the most common tools for interacting with learners.

SEVEN TIPS FOR WRITING FOR THE SCREEN

The third challenge of communicating online is adjusting your writing style to the screen, which presents several unique challenges of its own. One is writing content that is more likely to be scanned and skimmed—the usual reading pattern of online readers—than read in depth. A second is writing tightly because people typically do not read a lot of content on a single screen. The third is writing in dialogue with learners. A dialogue is preferred partly because reading online is an interactive

Table 9-1. Means of interacting with learners.

Means of Interacting	Symbol	Description
Checkboxes	☒	Let learners choose all the items on the list that apply to them
Radio buttons	○	Let learners choose one from a list when the list contains seven or fewer items
Drop-down list	▼	Let learners choose one item from a list when the list has eight or more items
Email	✉	Provide direct communication between the learner and the instructor
Entry fields		Provide a specific piece of information, whether a single word or an entire paragraph
Icons, links, and buttons	<u>Link</u>	Take learners to related information elsewhere in the learning program or outside the program

experience. It is also preferred because broadcast communication (one-way communication) is akin to lecturing, a method that is rarely advocated for classroom training, much less for e-learning.

The following sections suggest ways you can effectively address these issues when writing for the screen.

1. Write Good Leads

News writers know that readers decide whether to read a full article based on the first, or lead, paragraph. Writers therefore spend an exceptional amount of time crafting it. Similarly, developers of online learning programs know that learners determine whether to continue reading a topic based on the relevance communicated in the first paragraph.

Although it must also be engagingly written, a good lead paragraph must also give the main points—who, what, where, when, why, and how—and be succinct (35 words is ideal, 50 is a maximum).

Two popular ways to open a topic are explaining "What's in it for me?" (WIIFM) and linking the new content to information presented in the previous topic.

2. Write for Scanning and Skimming

Effective online communication takes advantage of the knowledge that online readers tend to scan text for relevant information and then skim the passages of interest.

Liberal use of headings—not just for the topic but for content within a topic—facilitates scanning.

Using charts and lists to present content facilitates skimming. Here are some tips for using lists:

- Start with a lead-in sentence.
- Only use numbers when the items on the list must be considered in the order in which they are presented, such as a description of a procedure or process. Otherwise, use bullets.
- Limit lists to seven items. If you have more than seven items, combine some into sublists, which are also called nested lists (because they are nested within a larger list).
- Limit nesting to one level.

3. Write Dialogue, Not Text

Although a computer is not a person, the interaction between humans and computers resembles a dialogue. The computer asks for information, and the learner responds. Based on the learner's response, the computer presents additional information.

Because the interaction resembles a dialogue, you need to write it as such. Specifically, you should write in the second person. That is, refer to learners as "you" (second person) rather than as "he or she," "they," or "the learner" (the third person). Use short sentences, sentence fragments, and one-word responses. For example, simply say "correct" to an answer and not "the response is correct."

4. Maintain a Positive Tone

At every level, educators try to motivate learners by taking a positive approach. In the classroom, that positive approach is often communicated through tone of voice. Online, that positive approach is communicated through the general tone of the text and visuals, and through the choice of words. Be sure to emphasize a positive tone when you provide feedback to incorrect responses. Use neutral words; for example, the term "not correct" is as clear as the term "wrong," but it carries less emotional impact.

5. Emphasize Precision and Clarity

Because instructors and learners are often separated by time and space, learners cannot immediately question material they don't understand, as they can in the classroom or in a synchronous online course. Similarly, this separation increases the likelihood that learners might misinterpret concepts or misread content. As a result, developers of online courses have an imperative to communicate clearly and precisely. Specific tips for writing clearly and precisely include these:

■ *Use parallelisms:* Parallelism means that you use an identical grammatical construction to explain similar concepts. Using a question-and-answer format for all of the headings in a chapter is an example of a parallelism.

■ *Consider the precise meanings of words:* We often use words interchangeably that, on closer inspection, really don't interchange all that well.

■ *Avoid vague expressions:* Expressions such as "there is," "there are," and "it is" do not refer to anything, making the task of comprehension harder for the reader.

■ *Avoid abbreviations:* Some abbreviations and acronyms can be misinterpreted, especially the ones that you think everyone in your organization already knows. If you must use an acronym or abbreviation, define it on the first use.

■ *Avoid the use of etc., i.e, and e.g.:* Style experts suggest using the terms *and so on, and so forth, that is,* and *such as.*

6. Avoid Assumptions

Even if learners understand the material presented, they sometimes adversely respond to the manner in which it is presented because it makes an unfair or incorrect assumption about them.

Don't make assumptions about the ease with which learners will grasp the content by using terms such as *easy, clear,* and *simple.* Just because you say so does not mean learners will find the material to be easy, clear, and simple. Rather, they learn at different rates and with varying degrees of ease.

Another pitfall is making assumptions about the learners' cultures. People often write from their own experience and inadvertently insert their culture into it. Cultures vary. Some cultural differences arise from differences in origin, such as people who are born and raised in different countries (even ones that speak the same language as you). As a result, conventions such as 10-digit telephone numbers, social security numbers, format for dates, colloquialisms, business buzzwords, and catch phrases may be unfamiliar.

Other cultural differences result from learners' occupations, industry, and social class. Consequently, examples that are intended to clarify material may not be helpful if they too closely resemble your own experience and do not resemble that of the learners.

7. Write Tightly

Tight writing means expressing a point in the fewest possible words. By doing so, you ensure an efficient delivery of content. One way to write tightly is to establish arbitrary limits for the length of content. For example, limit

■ sentences to 50 words
■ paragraphs to seven lines (studies indicate that the ideal paragraph length is five to seven lines)

- topics to one or two screens
- lessons (units) to 10–20 screens.

Although you'll need to exceed these limits in some instances, they will help you to keep your writing succinct.

Another way to write tightly is by cutting unnecessary words. See the companion Website for ways to tighten up your writing.

MAKING CHANGES TO THE PLANS

Invariably, as you develop the content, you will find that you need to diverge from the original plan. On the one hand, because the plan is just that, you should feel free to make changes as appropriate. See table 9-2 for ways to handle changes to your plans.

But, because the plan represents an agreement among the course developers and the sponsors, changes that are made without approval can, at the least, cause friction in the development effort. Because this plan was also used to develop schedules and budgets and because some changes might increase the workload, the changes have financial implications and the additional time must be approved before the change can be made.

Table 9-2. How to handle changes to your plan.

For This Type of Change:	Handle This Way:
A change in the method of presenting content that does not change the scope of the project (e.g., using an analogy instead of the example called for in the plan)	Contact the instructional designer (if that person is not you), who may choose to contact the sponsor.
A change in the method of presenting content that increases the scope of the project (that is, adds to the time or budget)	Prepare a revised storyboard along with an explanation of the change and an estimate of the additional resources needed. Submit to the instructional designer (if not you), who will submit it to management and the sponsor for approval.
A change in technical content that does not change the scope of the project	Ask the subject matter expert requesting the change to document the request in a memo.
A change in technical content that changes the scope of the project (adds to the time or budget)	First, ask the subject matter expert requesting the change to document the request in a memo. Then, only if the change is approved, prepare a revised storyboard along with an explanation of the change and an estimate of the additional resources needed. Submit to the instructional designer (if not you), who will submit it to management and the sponsor for approval.

YOUR TURN

In this chapter you learned how to communicate effectively with your learners online by taking advantage of the characteristics of the screen by communicating visually and interactively, and adjusting your writing style to the screen. How well you accomplish this affects the ultimate success of your online learning project. Now it is your turn to apply these concepts to your own project, or one you are planning to begin, using worksheet 9-1.

Worksheet 9-1. Checklist for developing online content.

Did you communicate visually?	1. Did you represent numerical data as: • pie charts (relating parts to the whole)? ☐ Yes ☐ No • bar charts or histograms (changes over time)? ☐ Yes ☐ No 2. Did you show relationships through organization charts? ☐ Yes ☐ No 3. Did you show things through photographs (pre-sales or primarily motivational content) or line drawings (post-sales or primarily instructional content)? ☐ Yes ☐ No 4. Did you represent processes through flow charts? ☐ Yes ☐ No 5. Did you represent concepts through symbols or icons? ☐ Yes ☐ No 6. Did you use graphics for instructional purposes rather than adornment? ☐ Yes ☐ No
Did you communicate interactively	1. Did you use interaction for quizzes, group exercises, or simulations? ☐ Yes ☐ No 2. Did you interact frequently with learners? ☐ Yes ☐ No 3. Did you provide appropriate feedback? ☐ Yes ☐ No 4. Did you use appropriate controls, such as radio buttons when learners must choose only one item from a list of seven or fewer items? ☐ Yes ☐ No

(continued on next page)

Worksheet 9-1. Checklist for developing online content (continued).

Did you write appropriately for the screen?	1. Did you write good leads? ☐ Yes ☐ No 2. Did you write for scanning and skimming? ☐ Yes ☐ No 3. Did you take a positive tone? ☐ Yes ☐ No 4. Did you emphasize precision and clarity in the choice of words? ☐ Yes ☐ No 5. Did you avoid assumptions about learners and the way they will perceive the content? ☐ Yes ☐ No 6. Did you write tightly? ☐ Yes ☐ No
Did you report changes?	1. For changes that involve a change in scope, did you receive approval from both the sponsor and instructional designer? ☐ Yes ☐ No 2. For changes that did not involve a change in scope, did you inform the instructional designer? Other members of the team? ☐ Yes ☐ No

10

Getting Technical and Editorial Reviews and Running Tests

One of the key challenges of preparing an online learning program is the imperative to get it right on the first try. When the program is made available to learners, it must be accurate and readable, and it must run without errors (such as "Error 404: Page not found"). Reviews and tests provide the most reliable means of ensuring that the online learning program possesses these qualities. This chapter describes the three categories of reviews performed for online learning programs:

- technical reviews, which assess the completeness and accuracy of the technical content
- editorial reviews, which assess the clarity of the writing along with the grammar, style, and consistency of the content
- technical tests, which assess whether the online learning program really works under everyday operating conditions.

This chapter describes the different types of reviews, suggests ways to perform them, and suggests how to respond to information learned in the tests.

In addition to these reviews and tests, developers should also conduct a usability test to make sure that learners actually learn the intended material from the program. Chapter 7 discusses usability tests.

TECHNICAL REVIEWS

Designers of online learning programs rely on the feedback of SMEs, marketing specialists, clients, and others to assess the completeness and accuracy of the program's content. The process by which these people read drafts and provide their assessments is called a review. Reviews are especially important for those online learning programs in which incorrect technical information could pose a potential liability such as the following:

- In regulated industries, such as the pharmaceutical industry, incorrect content could cause learners to perform their jobs incorrectly and that could create a life-threatening situation (such as doctor prescribing the wrong drug).
- For new products, such as software, that are not yet complete when development of the online learning program begins, the learning program could provide incorrect instructions, causing frustration and other potential problems for learners.
- Online learning programs in such fields as medicine or nuclear engineering may require specialized expertise beyond that of the course developer.
- Content for programs that have high visibility or sensitivity within the organization, such as management training, must represent a consensus viewpoint.

During a review, designated people read through the draft of a learning program and assess its effectiveness according to a set of criteria. The criteria vary according to the reviewer's perspective and expertise. For example, an SME can review a draft to assess whether the learning program is accurate. A marketing specialist can review a draft to assess whether the learning program is going to reach the intended audience. And, a sponsor can review a draft to assess whether the intended users will be able to achieve the intended objectives.

Learning programs are typically reviewed as part of the design process and after the first two drafts. Learning programs go through two types of technical reviews: informal and formal. During informal technical reviews, course developers ask close associates to review an early version of the learning product to assess whether it is "on track." Generally, one or two course developers and a trusted SME conduct informal reviews on early versions of drafts, before they are sent for formal reviews to catch showstoppers that might damage the credibility of the course developer. For formal technical reviews, course developers invite all stakeholders within the organization to provide feedback on the completeness and accuracy of a draft. Usually several people simultaneously review a draft.

The Informal Technical Review

As mentioned earlier, an informal review is one in which course developers ask close and trusted associates to review an early version of a learning program to assess whether it is on track. Through this assessment, you catch major technical flaws and learn which aspects work and which ones need formal work. As a result, you can respond to the feedback before you send the draft for wide review in the organization and maintain your credibility within your organization.

Note that informal reviews are not formally scheduled and are conducted in addition to the formal reviews that are scheduled. Some issues to consider when planning an informal review:

- Solicit feedback as early as possible. The best time is immediately after you finish the draft—before you have had a chance to become emotionally invested in the work. If you need to make changes, you will feel less emotionally resistant to doing so. (No one likes to learn that a draft must be completely rewritten, but the more time you invest in crafting and reworking a draft before receiving feedback, the worse that feeling is. An informal review can spare you some of that emotional pain.)

- Conduct the review before the formal review is scheduled. In this way, you can make changes and send a more polished draft to reviewers.

- Identify people who will be effective reviewers. See the sidebar, "How to Choose Informal Reviewers" for details.

- Send friendly reminders to reviewers during the review period. Despite their best intentions, many reviewers do not complete the assignment unless prodded to do so and provided with a due date.

> ## How to Choose Informal Reviewers
>
> **C**arefully choose your informal reviewer. Choose someone you trust, who knows the sponsor and the target learners, and who is willing to devote the time it takes to do a careful review. The reviewer should be someone
>
> - *whom you trust:* You need to trust the informal reviewer's skill in assessing learning products as well as this person's ability to provide you with feedback and advice that will ultimately benefit you.
> - *who knows the sponsor:* The informal reviewer can offer insights into the sponsor's likely reaction to your work.
> - *who knows the learners:* The informal reviewer can also offer insights into the likely reaction of learners to your presentation of content.
> - *who has the time:* The informal reviewer needs to read closely enough to identify any major flaws in the technical content and how it is presented, whether it reaches the learner, and how well it meets the sponsors' needs. Although the informal review is not included in the project schedule, contact informal reviewers in advance to make sure they have time to dedicate to your review.

The Formal Technical Review

Because few reviewers have "reviewer" in their job descriptions and, as a result, may not know what is expected of them when they perform a review, many need coaching from you to provide you with the feedback you need. The best way to provide this coaching is by approaching the review process in an organized manner.

Plan. The first step in the formal technical review is planning for it. Advance planning helps you make sure that the right people have the opportunity to review your drafts and that they have enough time to provide helpful feedback. Follow these steps to plan a successful formal review:

1. Determine who should review the online learning program. Ultimately, you want many perspectives on the draft so that the information is considered from every possible angle, yet not so many perspectives that you become overwhelmed. Most online learning programs benefit from reviews by SMEs, marketing specialists, and other representatives of the sponsor.

2. Plan sufficient time for the review into your schedule. Often, drafts are poorly reviewed because no one provided reviewers with enough time to review. The whole process including mailing, copying of drafts, distribution of drafts, and the return of drafts could take up to two weeks. Schedule at least one day at each end of the review for these administrative matters, another day for a review meeting, at least two days for the first 50 to 75 screens, and one day for each additional 50 to 75 screens. See the companion Website (http://saulcarliner .home.att.net/oll/index.html) for more details on scheduling a review.

3. Make certain that reviewers can review the draft at the scheduled time. Show reviewers the proposed schedule in advance and ask them for a commitment to meet the deadline for review. If they cannot meet your schedules, negotiate ones that work for them and still provide you sufficient time to prepare revisions based on the review comments.

Conduct the Review. Provide reviewers with complete drafts that are clearly marked *DRAFT* on each page. What do *complete* and *draft* really mean? Complete means that the version contains all the intended information. You call your credibility with reviewers into question when you provide reviewers with incomplete drafts (unless you have reached a prior agreement with them on this point). A complete draft includes every section and drafts of all graphics to be used. Avoid comments such as "to be added at the next draft."

Draft indicates that the online learning program is not yet ready for publication. By indicating that the program is only a draft, reviewers do not confuse it with a finished online learning program and are more likely to provide comments. In addition to marking each page prominently with the word *DRAFT*, you can also help reviewers by printing the draft in courier type (typewriter font). This choice of font encourages reviewers to focus more on technical content than on screen design. Because the draft looks like something that came from a typewriter, reviewers expect the screen design to change and focus their attention instead on the content—right where you want them to focus.

Send a cover letter with the draft to coach reviewers in their work and ask them to cover specific issues or check for information accuracy, a specific date to return the draft (without a return date, most reviewers will not respond in a timely manner), and directions on how to comment on the draft. See the companion Website (http://saulcarliner.home.att.net/oll/index.html) for a sample cover letter.

Formally Respond to Comments. After technical reviewers complete their work, they return comments to you. Because they have invested time and effort in their reviews of the draft, technical reviewers usually want to know whether you intend to incorporate their suggestions. As the course developer, you make the ultimate decision about how to handle the comments but are obligated to respond to each reviewer's comments.

For every comment that you receive, indicate one of the following:

■ accept (usually with a check mark, requires no additional comment)

■ reject (briefly explain why in a few words)

■ request clarification or additional information for comments that raise issues beyond your ability to resolve, such as how a particular engineering change will be implemented or a toll-free number that has not yet been assigned to a marketing campaign. For open issues like these, indicate when a resolution is needed so the project can move forward.

You respond to review comments in one of two ways. Some people write responses on the draft with the comments and send that back to the reviewer. Others schedule a review meeting. The meeting can be informal (just you and reviewer) or formal (all of the reviewers attend with a formal moderator to lead the proceedings). At the review meeting, participants identify major concerns and attempt to resolve them, such as comments that conflict with one another. Do not use this time to discuss corrections that can be made with the change of a sentence or two. See the companion Website for tips on conducting review meetings, as well as more detailed suggestions for responding to comments on technical reviews.

The Walk-Through, A Special Type of Review

In some instances, a reading review, in which reviewers read through the draft and write comments, does not elicit the extent of feedback that you need to ensure the accuracy of the learning program. In such instances, you would consider conducting a series of walk-throughs.

In a walk-through, reviewers use the meeting time to read through the draft. This type of review is conducted only with printed drafts, even for online materials. The group "walks through" each page of the draft, and participants make their comments at that time. If a difference of opinion arises, the group resolves it then. Walk-throughs are especially useful in these instances:

■ processes for which the course developer does not have access to prototypes

■ abstract processes, such as troubleshooting, for which no single correct procedure exists

■ instances in which SMEs have a history of conducting lax reviews, and the only way to get reviews from them is by "locking them in a room."

Prepare for a walk-through in much the same way that you prepare for other formal review meetings, but with one important difference. For walk-throughs, schedule a series of meetings, one for each unit, rather than a single meeting to address all of them. In addition, schedule walk-through meetings to last for three to four hours, rather than 90 minutes. You should conduct the walk-throughs on consecutive days for a period of one or two weeks, rather than stretching them out over a longer time.

EDITORIAL REVIEWS

An editor serves as the "first reader" of a communication product. As the first reader, the editor addresses a wide range of issues that, if not addressed, could cause problems for readers. Many people are familiar with the more basic of these issues, pertaining to grammar, usage, spelling, punctuation, and other mechanical aspects of text. This task of making sure that copy is grammatically and stylistically correct is called copyediting.

Editors also serve a more substantive role, working closely with course developers to fortify the structure of an online learning program, to identify and resolve unclear passages, and to enhance the presentation of information so that learners can easily understand it. This communication coaching, called substantive editing, is one of the key benefits that an editor brings to an online learning program.

Under ideal circumstances, editors review each draft of an online learning program. The nature of their comments varies depending on the stage of the draft. As the draft moves from concept to committed prose, the breadth of focus moves from broad issues of presentation to specific issues of style and grammar. Comments on earlier drafts are primarily substantive. Comments on later drafts are primarily copyedits. Because editors review drafts at different levels of depth, the different types of editing are called levels of editing.

The First Draft: A Substantive Edit

In a substantive edit, the editor suggests ways that course developers can more effectively craft the learning program. Comments may suggest restructuring of entire units, rewording of large passages to better match the level of audience, or replacing a long section of text with a chart. Specifically, editors look for the following at the first draft:

- Is the organization clear? If not, what is unclear? How could the organization be strengthened so that learners can better understand it?
- Are units clear? Does one point logically flow to the next? Do the points make sense? If not, how could points flow more naturally and be expressed more clearly?
- Are there logic gaps in the information? (Technical reviewers indicate if technical content is missing.) If so, what are the gaps? How might the developer fill the gap?
- Could information be expressed in another way? If so, how? How would changing the presentation improve the learning program?

■ Is the content consistent in tone and style from unit to unit? Is this program consistent with similar online learning programs? Does the content in one part complement or contradict content in another part? How can the course developer resolve the inconsistency?

Although editors do not focus on issues of grammar and style at this draft, if they see a problem, they usually note it. When addressing these issues of grammar and style, editors consult the dictionary and style guide that you designated when you set the editorial guidelines for the project.

If you are following editorial conventions that are not indicated in the style guide or dictionary, you should provide the editor with your project-specific style guide with the review draft. As the style guide grows, provide a revised version with each draft. Tell the editor what has changed since the last draft, or the changes may be overlooked.

The Second Draft: Crafting the Copy

Editorial reviews at this point focus on mechanical matters; you may need to restructure individual paragraphs, clarify parts of an illustration, or rewrite particular sentences. Specific issues that editors consider at the second draft include the following:

■ *Structure of units:* Editors often review the headings within a section to see if they are parallel to one another. Unparallel headings within a section often indicate a structural problem.

■ *Clarity:* Are all terms and concepts adequately defined? If not, how can they be clarified?

■ *Consistency:* Do points made in one section concur or conflict with points in others? Did you use terminology consistently? Did you use like expressions to express like concepts and instructions?

■ *Appropriateness and clarity of graphics:* Do graphics convey concepts, enhance the meaning of the text, or merely adorn the learning product? Similarly, would a graphic more effectively communicate an idea than text?

■ *Transitions among points:* Does one screen easily flow to the next? If not, what transitions should you add to improve the flow?

Editors also begin to focus on issues of grammar and style at this draft and identify inconsistencies in screen design, such as screens that do not follow the templates established earlier and graphics for which you have not provided captions.

The Third Draft: A Copyedit

At the third draft, the information becomes more solid and changes more costly to make. Therefore, editorial reviews focus almost exclusively on mechanical issues of grammar and style. Issues that editors consider at the third draft include usage, spelling, punctuation, capitalization, consistency of terminology, heading consistency, page and screen design issues, template and navigation bar consistency, table and chart consistency, placement of illustrations and graphics, and margin and type font issues.

Responding to Editorial Comments

Respond to editorial comments in much the same way that you respond to technical review comments: Go through the commented drafts and indicate on the page whether you intend to incorporate the comment. If you do plan to incorporate the comment, briefly explain why.

As a unique aspect of the process for providing feedback, editors often meet with course developers to discuss the comments. This meeting is called an author-editor conference. This meeting substantially differs from a review meeting in its informality and its collaborative tone. Some editors prefer to give their comments to authors at this meeting, so that editors have a chance to explain the comments before authors consider them. Other editors prefer to deliver the comments first and meet later with the author to answer questions and discuss the edits.

TECHNICAL TESTS

Tests ensure that an online learning program actually works when running on a computer. They verify that the links and branches in an online learning program work as designed, that the program runs when integrated with other components and software, and that the program can handle the number of users at one time that it was designed to handle.

The tests are typically scheduled after all development of the online learning program is complete and its content is unlikely to change. Specifically, you perform the following tests on an online learning program. The tests are usually conducted in the sequence in which they are presented here.

1. Functional Test

Functional tests verify that each link and branch works as designed. Specifically, this test ensures the following:

- Each option on the navigation bar on each screen takes learners to the designated place. For example, does clicking on "menu" really bring up a menu and clicking on "back" really send learners back one screen?
- Each response to a question brings up the appropriate feedback. For example, does choosing answer *a* for a multiple choice question bring up the feedback to choice *a,* or choice *b*?
- Each link in the program directs learners to the designated page. For example, if the course has a link to an online reference, does it really link there or has the Web address (URL) moved?

■ All media elements operate as expected. That is, does the video (usually shot and edited separately from the rest of the online learning program) operate as expected when integrated into the program?

For short programs, people conduct their own functional tests. But for longer ones, many course developers work with others to conduct these tests. In some cases, programmers write routines that automatically check these options. Some firms also sell software that automatically checks links. In other cases, course developers hire others to conduct the tests manually (often interns). And, in still other cases, course developers use a combination of approaches.

Note that all tests, including the functional test, should be conducted on a system that meets the minimum configuration for viewing the program to ascertain that it really works on such a system. You can also test the program on systems that exceed these minimum requirements to see if the differences create unanticipated problems.

2. Integration Test

To verify that the online learning program works when other programs are running on the computer, an integration test is carried out. One of the specific issues for this test is verifying that the online learning program operates with all of the browsers for which it is designed. For example, if the online learning program is supposed to operate under Netscape Navigator versions 4.6 and 6.0 and Microsoft Internet Explorer versions 4.0 and 5.0, does it really operate under all of these? Typically, an integration test is conducted manually.

3. Load Test

The load test confirms that the online learning program can handle a given number of learners at the same time. For example, if the online learning program is supposed to handle 30 simultaneous learners, can it actually handle them? With how many programs loaded? If the program cannot handle the requisite number of learners running other necessary software, then something must be adjusted.

A load test is only needed for online learning programs run off a server. It helps developers assess how many learners can gain access to the program before one is "locked out," that is, not able to get gain access to the learning program.

Responding to the Test Results

These tests identify what's working and what needs to be fixed before the program is ready to be published.

Problems uncovered through testing are assigned priorities. Typically, issues raised are usually categorized as follows:

■ *A:* a showstopper, which must be fixed immediately or development cannot continue

- *B:* a must-fix problem, which won't hold up program development but must be addressed before the online learning program is released
- *C:* a low-priority problem, either because the change is not essential or requires more work than can be done before the scheduled publication of the program.

When responding to the issues raised by the test, prepare an action plan that lists the following:

- issues to be addressed
- priority (*A, B,* or *C*)
- corrective action to be taken
- deadline for completing the corrective action
- person responsible for taking the corrective action.

The action plan is typically published within two to three business days of completing a test, and is usually followed up a week or two later. See the accompanying Website for a sample of an action plan.

YOUR TURN

This chapter discussed the three types of reviews for an online learning program. It is through these reviews that you determine if the text that appears in your program is technically accurate, clear and grammatically correct, and whether it works as advertised.

Now, it's your turn to apply these concepts to your own project or to one you are planning, using worksheet 10-1. Consider the types of reviews and tests that your learning program will entail. Whom might you tap to serve as editors, reviewers, testers, and SMEs to carry out the reviews and tests? Do you anticipate that walk-through reviews might be necessary in some cases?

Worksheet 10-1. A plan for conducting reviews and tests of your e-learning program.

Draft	Reviews/Tests	Reviewers/Editors/SMEs	Schedule (Date Out for Review, Date to Return Comments)
First	Technical review		
	Editorial review		
	Test: Usability test		
Second	Technical review		
	Editorial review		

	Tests:
	  Usability test
	  Functional test		

Third	Technical review		
	Editorial review		

	Tests:
	  Functional test
	  Integration test
	  Load test		

Preparation for Final Draft	Copyedit		

	Tests:
	  Functional test
	  Integration test
	  Load test		

11

Preparing for Final Production

Production is the process of readying a learning program for publication online, and its accompanying materials for publication online or in print. This chapter describes the three main tasks involved in converting your draft materials into a cohesive package that's suitable for publication. These tasks include

- preparing the components of the online learning program
- creating a single master online learning package
- distributing the online learning program.

TASK 1: PREPARE THE COMPONENTS OF THE ONLINE LEARNING PROGRAM

The first step in the production process is converting the drafts of the various elements you have developed into pieces that can be combined into a master copy. The exact pieces that you prepare vary depending upon the various media used in your online learning program, but they are likely to include graphics, video, and audio sequences, as well as complex programming. In addition, you have the entire package copyedited, and you prepare front and back matter. The next several sections describe these activities.

Copyedit Text Intended for Publication

Copyediting is the process of marking text for final typesetting. Copyediting begins after the sponsor has approved all of the text and released it for publication. As mentioned in chapter 10, the copyeditor looks for grammar and style errors and legal issues. Additionally, he or she makes sure that the production staff has adequate instructions for producing the learning program.

Prepare the Front and Back Matter

In addition to the content for the online learning program, you must also provide a variety of other information to introduce and conclude the program. Introductory material is called *front matter* because it appears at the beginning of the program. Concluding material is called *back matter*, because it appears at the end. If this material has not been prepared earlier, it must be at this stage of program development.

Much of the front and back matter of an online learning program is standard and does not require original writing. In fact, preparing some of the components of the front or back matter feels like filling in the blanks. In other cases, it involves assembling material that is available elsewhere.

Preparing the front matter involves the following tasks:

■ *Preparing the title screen:* Make sure you include the name of the online learning program and the publisher.

■ *Preparing an edition notice:* This section provides copyright and other legal information and is usually placed at the bottom of the title screen.

■ *Writing a preface:* This section describes the purpose, background, intended audience, and scope of information within the online learning program. Learners scan the preface to determine whether the program meets their needs, if any printed instructional material is needed, and if the computer equipment or network being used is sufficient for the online learning program. The information in the preface should also be reflected in the program's promotional material.

■ *Providing other relevant background information:* List any conventions used in the program or instructions for taking the course.

■ *Preparing the main menu:* The main menu lists all of the major sections in the online learning program. In some instances, the main menu only lists the primary topics. In other cases, it lists both the primary and secondary topics.

Preparing the back matter involves the following tasks:

■ *Creating appendixes:* Appendixes contain material that expands upon the content but is not mandatory to achieve the learning objectives. Create appendixes if a need exists and be sure that the text makes appropriate references to them.

■ *Preparing a glossary:* Learners appreciate glossaries when they encounter a word they think they should know but can't remember its definition. Linking these words in the body of the program is also a good idea.

■ *Creating an index:* Some learners prefer this method over a menu.

■ *Developing a level 1 learner satisfaction survey:* The main purpose of the survey is to find out whether the e-learning program met the learners' needs. You can also use the survey to solicit ideas for improving the program.

■ *Adding links:* These links direct the learner to related programs and materials (if appropriate).

See the companion Website (http://saulcarliner.home.att.net/oll/index.html) for detailed instructions for preparing most components of the front and back matter, and samples of them.

Produce Graphics

As you prepare for production, you convert images from ideas to concrete graphics. If you are using clip art and other types of previously created images, or if you are skilled in creating graphics, you may have already prepared the graphics while developing earlier drafts of the learning program. But if you are using photographs or hiring a graphic artist to prepare images, you will most likely wait until the sponsor approves the final version of the online learning program product before hiring the specialists needed to produce these images. (If you hire them earlier in the process and the content changes, you may waste funds.)

The activities for producing graphics depend on the types of images used in your online learning program. You may need to prepare original drawings, such as line drawings and icons, or specialized images, such as three-dimensional drawings. Alternatively, you can add graphic touches—lines, shading, special typography—to text.

Graphics production may also involve photography. Consider hiring a professional for best results. Although you can find seemingly foolproof, point-and-shoot cameras, you should hire a photographer to take photographs for you. Simple photography is primary intended for personal use. Industrial photography, while not as elaborate as magazine and fashion photography, still requires extensive attention to lighting, placement of images, and other details—skills requiring a professional photographer.

Furthermore, if you intend to include people in your photographs, you need to consider such issues as hiring and preparing models, and using model release forms. A professional photographer can assist you with these issues, too.

After taking the photograph, the photographer, a graphic artist, or you can retouch it using special software. Your options include the following:

- Choose to print a small part of the photograph. The process of removing parts of the photograph is called cropping.
- Remove unnecessary details, such as an arm that is not attached to any person in the photograph.
- Change the image size.
- Remove blemishes, such as a blemish on someone's face.
- Enhance the shading and colors.
- Add visual effects, such as effects that make the photograph appear to be ancient or look like a drawing.

You may also consider adapting drawings from other sources. When you adapt a drawing, you can

- add or remove features (such as adding color)
- change the size of the image
- crop the drawing, which involves cutting off part of the image and changing the image size.

In some cases, you can hire an artist to prepare a basic image and add or remove features from it. In other cases, you can scan a picture into the computer from another source, such as a book or photograph and, using graphics or photo refinishing software, add and remove features and crop it.

Produce and Edit Audiovisual Components

Audiovisual components, which include narration, background music, and video sequences, are the most complex to produce because they usually involve an entire production crew that has had little involvement with the project until this point. Depending on the component and the sophistication of the production, the time needed to produce these elements may be extensive; in some cases, as long as is needed to produce the information.

Production processes vary, too, for audio and video sequences. The following sections provide an overview of the production processes.

Producing Audio Sequences. Producing audio sequences usually involves the following tasks:

1. Hire a sound engineer. Although, you can find easy-to-operate recording equipment, this equipment is usually intended for personal use. When producing industrial quality audio, you need to control background noise and noise levels; you may even need to record the script out of sequence and piece—or edit—it back together. You may also need to add sound effects and background music. A sound engineer can perform these tasks.
2. Reserve a studio. Studios have the recording equipment built in and are specially built to block out background noise. The sound engineer can reserve the studio for you.
3. Verify the narration. Ask someone to read through the script, and then rewrite awkward expressions and provide phonetic spellings of difficult-to-pronounce words.
4. Hire a professional narrator. To do so, contact a local talent agency and ask them to send over a demo tape with brief recordings from several prospective narrators. Identify the ones who have the vocal qualities you seek, then ask for a longer tape. From that group, choose a narrator. Tell the talent agency, and then they will work with you to schedule the narrator and arrange for payment. Wages are likely to be set by a local talent union. Invite sponsors to help choose a narrator because that voice represents them to the public. (Although you can use an amateur who has a good voice, a professional narrator can usually record a script in one or two takes, requiring less of the expensive studio time than an amateur does.)
5. Record the narration. The sound engineer manages this process. You should be present, however, to provide technical assistance and approve any last-minute rewrites.

6. Edit the audio. The sound engineer takes care of this task. First, the sound engineer takes the specific sequences that you preferred and places them in proper sequence. For example, perhaps you liked the recording of paragraph 1 from the first recording but preferred paragraphs 2 and 3 from the second recording. The sound engineer can take those sequences and arrange them in order.

7. Add audio enhancements. Next, the sound engineer adds sound effects and background music. The sound engineer should ask for your approval on both before using them. The use of computerized sound equipment lets the sound engineer easily prepare sound out of sequence. The sound engineer also makes sure that you have approval to use copyrighted sounds.

8. Perform audio checks. After editing the pieces of audio together, the sound engineer reviews the entire recording for sound quality. If the sound levels in one part are higher than in another, the sound engineer adjusts the sound quality. Various types of meters help the sound engineer measure and adjust sound quality.

9. Prepare the master recording. The recording might be on tape or disk, depending on your needs and the capabilities of the sound studio.

Producing Video Sequences. Producing video sequences involves the following:

1. Hire a professional director. Directors are best at spotting issues that need to be addressed in shooting, efficient at acquiring and using resources, and can hire quickly any special talent that's needed.

2. Prepare storyboards. A storyboard is a sequence of boards created by the director (not the course designer or developer) that indicates what the video will look and sound like. (These storyboards are produced in addition to the ones you produced as part of the design process.) The storyboard indicates every video shot needed, so the director can plan effectively for shooting.

3. Hire a production crew. The director hires a crew to assist with various aspects of shooting the video, such as lighting and sound assistants, props assistants, and floating assistants.

4. Reserve shooting locations. Because a location cannot be used for both shooting video and performing other types of work, you must reserve the site well in advance. If you plan to shoot in a work location, the person managing that location will likely request that you shoot the video after hours to avoid interrupting work. If you plan to shoot in a public place, you need the permission of the location owner and may need to pay a rental fee. If you plan to use a video studio (where you have the greatest control over sound and light), you need to reserve the space for your exclusive use. You must make separate reservations for each shooting location.

5. Hire on-screen talent, such as narrators and actors. The director has responsibility for hiring on-screen talent, but he or she should include you in the decisions.

6. Record and edit the video. The director records the various video sequences in the most efficient order, rather than in sequence. For example, because setting up the lighting and sound equipment takes so much time, if you use one location for two separate scenes, the director shoots both scenes at the same time to avoid a separate setup. You may wish to sit on the set during video shooting, but be prepared for a slow, tedious process. The director might take an hour or two just to get the lighting correct for a three-minute scene and then the scene may need to be shot several times until the reading is correct.

7. Edit the video. A video editor, sometimes called a producer, handles this task while working under the guidance of the director. As with sound recording, the video editor first takes the specific shots and places them in proper sequence. Next, the video editor adds sound effects and background music to the audio track. The video editor then adds visual effects, such as graphics (which are produced as the video sequences are shot), displayed words (which are produced at the time they are edited in), and transitions between scenes. For example, the editor can add a wipe, which wipes away one scene and introduces a next, or a fade, which fades down the visual image of one scene as the next one comes up.

8. Review the recording. After editing the pieces of video and sound together, the video editor reviews the entire recording for visual and sound quality. Using equipment similar to that of the sound engineer, the video editor adjusts sound quality if the sound levels in one part are higher than in another and adjusts picture quality if it is uneven. Various types of meters help the producer measure and adjust sound quality.

9. Prepare the master recording. The video editor then completes the work and prepares the master recording. The recording might be on tape or disk, depending on your needs and the capabilities of the sound studio. Preparing the master recording on disk might involve condensing the file by removing unnecessary information so that it requires the least amount of space.

Get Permission to Use Copyrighted Material

Make sure that you have written permission to publish all of the material in your online learning program. If the text, photograph, or illustration was previously published by your organization, verify that your organization owns all of the copyrights. In most cases, even if the work was prepared by an outside firm, your organization owns the copyright. But, photographs, graphics, and other visual materials might require additional permission. Check with the person in your organization who is responsible for the original publication to verify whether your organization owns the copyright and, if not, who does.

If your organization did not previously publish the material, you need to request permission for the following:

- Any text passages exceeding 250 words. For passages directly quoted and less than 250 words, you merely need to cite the source.
- Photographs (even ones that you commissioned or used from clip art or stock photo houses; they generally require a written permission)
- Clip art, stock sound, and stock video. Some clip art publishers require a fee for clips used in widely published materials, like online learning programs. The printed material that accompanies the clip art will tell you whether or not you need to seek permission.

When requesting permission, write to the owner of the copyright and tell them exactly which material you want to use. State the name of the publication, the number of intended readers, the planned date of publication, and the name of the publisher. Finally, state how the owner can contact you by mail. You need an original, signed letter granting permission. Some organizations charge a permissions fee to use their copyrighted material.

Finally, after you have received permission, provide the following documentation in the learning program: "From [source name]. [Full bibliographic information]. Used with permission." Your style guide will likely provide exact formatting guidance that you can use to ensure consistency from citation to citation. Here's an example:

From Barnum, Carol, and Carliner, Saul (editors). (1993). *Techniques for Technical Communicators*. New York: Prentice-Hall. Used with permission.

In addition to verifying permission to use copyrighted material, you must also mark trademarks. Many organizations register trademarks for names and phrases used in their business to prevent others from adopting these product and service names. Whether they belong to your organization or another, trademarked terms must be properly labeled on their first use in the online learning program. Some organizations list these terms in the edition notice (a part of the front matter). If you fail to indicate your own trademarks, your organization will have difficulty protecting them against unauthorized use.

Task 2: Combine the Elements Into a Single Master Package

With the various elements of the communication product now ready, incorporate them into a single package. Here is an overview of the steps involved in this activity:

1. Complete preparation of the text. Incorporate copyedits and integrate front and back matter, if you have not already done so.
2. Using your authoring tool, integrate the text, graphics, audio, and video. For example, if an audio sequence plays in the middle of a tutorial, indicate the name and location of that file in the master file for the online learning program.
3. Add other user interaction, if you have not already done so. At this point, make sure that all links, menus, search tools, answer analysis, branching, and

jumps to other types of media are available. For example, if you ask questions, you need to create the programming for users to answer those questions, and for the system to provide users with the appropriate responses. If the authoring tool will not let you create the type of interaction intended, create macros and other programs to overcome these limitations. A programmer may be needed to create these macros and programs.

4. Although it requires a separate production effort, create any workbooks, packaging, and related materials that accompany the online learning program, and arrange for printing if they are not going to be available online. The exact materials that you need will vary depending on the type of program that you are producing. For example, if you are preparing a CD-ROM or DVD, you need packaging and labels for the disk and, perhaps, a user's guide. If you are distributing material through the Web, you may produce marketing materials and flyers to promote the program. See the companion Website for more information on supporting materials.

5. Complete the following tests: (1) functional test (which makes sure that the program works as intended), (2) integration test (which makes sure that the program works when other programs are running), and (3) load test (only performed for materials distributed through a server to make sure that the designated number of learners can simultaneously take the learning program).

6. For online learning materials that need to be installed on a hard drive, develop, test, and document the installation program, which should be easy, fast, and intuitive for the learner. See the companion Website for more details on preparing an installation program.

7. Check for viruses, so that you do not distribute "contaminated" information to users.

8. Make at least one backup copy of the entire learning program, including separate pieces that might be printed. If anything happens to the original, you have a duplicate to work with.

9. If you are posting content on the Web, you can upload it to the Website at this time, or, if you are publishing CDs or DVDs, you submit the content to the duplication service. As part of this effort, you prepare a cover letter to accompany the package containing the master and related materials. The cover letter must stipulate the number of CDs or DVDs in the master, the number of CDs or DVDs in the final package (if different), packaging specifications, deadline for the job, shipping information, and any other instructions. An example of a cover letter appears on the companion Website (http://saulcarliner.home.att.net/oll/index.html).

10. The duplication service produces the printed materials such as labels, duplicates the program onto the CDs or DVDs (a process called writing or burning, because the information is literally burned onto the surface of the disk),

packages the pieces together, and wraps them (usually in plastic, called shrink wrapping).

11. The external service duplicates and ships the CDs and DVDs in their packaging.

Task 3: Distribute the Online Learning Program

After duplicating the communication product, it is ready to distribute to the intended users. In some cases, course developers are responsible for distributing their programs, but it is more usual for someone else within the organization to do so. Table 11-1 describes the two most common methods of distributing online learning programs. See the companion Website for a description of other options.

Table 11-1. Distribution pointers.

If You Are Distributing on...	What You Need in the Production Package
CD-ROM or DVD	• The user's guide, even if it's just a brochure with instructions on how to insert the diskettes into the diskette drive • CD or DVD labels • A sample package for the printer
Server or World Wide Web	The master copy that is already online is actually all ready for distribution to users. But, you need to consider two additional steps: • Choose and test a firewall program to prevent unauthorized users from gaining access. • Make sure marketing materials tell the primary learners how to gain access to the e-learning program.

Your Turn

This chapter explained how to prepare your online learning program for publication. It explained how to prepare content for production through copyediting, preparation of front and back matter, preparation of graphics, and video and audio production, and receiving permission to use copyrighted material. Then, it explained how to create a master copy of the online learning package, and distribute it to learners. Now, using worksheet 11-1, take some time to see if you have addressed all these points in planning for your online learning program.

Worksheet 11-1. Consider the steps you need to take to prepare for final production.

Task	Checklist
Task 1: Prepare the Components of the Online Learning Program	Copyedit text ☐ Yes ☐ No Prepare front and back matter ☐ Title screen ☐ Main menu ☐ Glossary ☐ Preface ☐ Index ☐ Satisfaction Form ☐ Edition notice ☐ Appendixes Produce graphics ☐ Yes ☐ No Produce and edit audiovisual components ☐ Yes ☐ No Verify permission to use copyrighted material ☐ Yes ☐ No
Task 2: Combine the Elements into a Single "Master" Package	Complete preparation of the text ☐ Yes ☐ No Integrate the text with graphics, audio, and video ☐ Yes ☐ No Make sure that all links, menus, indexes, search tools, answer analysis, branching, and "jumps" to other types of media are available ☐ Yes ☐ No Produce and print any workbooks, packaging, or related materials ☐ Yes ☐ No Complete functional testing ☐ Yes ☐ No Develop, test, and document the installation program ☐ Yes ☐ No
Task 3: Distribute the Online Learning Program	Perform virus scan ☐ Yes ☐ No Prepare a backup copy of the e-learning program ☐ Yes ☐ No Submit program file to duplication service or upload to server ☐ Yes ☐ No Assemble your production package ☐ User's guide ☐ CD/DVD labels ☐ Sample package for printer Ensure that firewall protection is in place for online distribution ☐ Yes ☐ No Prepare marketing materials that tell learners how to access the learning program ☐ Yes ☐ No

12

Launching, Supporting, and Maintaining the Learning Program

Even if you have created a great online learning program, you still have to let the world know that it exists, and be prepared to assist learners when they start taking it. This chapter explains how to do so. Specifically, it suggests ways to promote new and existing online learning programs, then discusses issues to consider when supporting and maintaining them, and last, briefly describes issues to consider when closing an online learning project.

LAUNCHING AN ONLINE LEARNING PROGRAM

To get your product to the learners, you must promote it. The following sections highlight just a few ways to put the spotlight on your online learning program.

Collateral Material

First, you need to have clear, accurate descriptions of your learning program, and you must state the benefits for potential learners. This information is often called collateral material because it is essential to the promotion of the course, and is included in any print or online catalog of learning programs. The description should accurately represent the course and do the following:

- provide a 50–75 word description of the course (begin with an action verb to help keep on track)
- state the objectives of the course
- describe the intended audience
- identify prerequisites (although typically stated as course titles, you provide more help to learners by stating the skills they should have mastered before starting the learning program, then state the courses that teach those skills, such as "you should be able to use the mouse, as taught in "Mouse Essentials"")

- state the number of modules
- estimate the time needed to complete the course.

Figure 12-1 shows an example of a course description.

Other collateral material includes links to the course description in other online content, such as online help, the technical support Website, and the corporate marketing site. Collateral material might also include mentions in printed materials, such as user's guides, other product documentation, and business cards (at least include a link to the site where the program is available).

Finally, collateral material includes the packaging for the online learning program if it is separately packaged as a CD or DVD. The packaging for the program should have a design that encourages people to pick it up, and the accompanying text on the package should invite people to try the program.

Figure 12-1. An example of a course description for an online learning program.

DEVELOPING PERFORMANCE SUPPORT AND AGENT-BASED SYSTEMS

Length:
Ten 1-hour modules

About This Course
Shows you how to develop intelligent agents such as wizards and intelligent tutors. Specifically, this course investigates the performance, usability, technical, and editorial considerations involved in designing different types of agents, and provides opportunities to design your own. It also explains how to coordinate these agents with more traditional communication products in a comprehensive performance improvement campaign. Finally, this course presents anticipated developments in the agent technology.

Objectives
Main Objective: Include agents in either a help system or an interface.

Supporting Objectives: To achieve the main objective, you should be able to:
- Name the most common types of agents.
- Define performance support systems.
- Describe the performance considerations underlying the choice of agents.
- Describe guidelines for ensuring usable agents.
- Describe the two general approaches to coding intelligent interface agents.
- Describe costs to include in the estimates of a knowledge-based product.
- Name potential sources of liability and exposure from the use of agents.
- Explain how to tie together agents in a communication campaign.

Who Should Attend:
Information designers, information developers, instructional designers, Web developers, usability engineers, and others who have developed at least five online communication products

Other Promotional Materials

Promotional material raises awareness of a course in the short run and is only intended to have a shelf life of four to eight weeks. Promotional material can take many forms, including flyers about the course, posters, and banner ads on corporate Websites (including intranet sites). You can announce or promote the course via email messages, which usually are sent to participants in previous courses or people who fit the demographic profile of the intended learners.

Build Appropriate Expectations

When developing promotional materials, make sure that they realistically represent the program. One of the challenges of introducing online learning is building appropriate expectations. Some of the key expectations to manage are the following:

- *Length:* Although some people like to use a formula to estimate the length of an online learning program, such as 1 screen = 1 minute, the truth is that the average length of time varies, depending on the density of the text on the screen, the length of any video or animation sequences, the complexity of the content, and the quality of the presentation. Consequently, you should time several users before stating the time. Choose a time that is realistic for at least 85 or 90 percent of the users, which is longer than the average time. If you only state the average time, half of the learners will take more time to complete the program and that could leave them feeling discouraged, and cause them to drop out.
- *Interactivity:* Most online learning programs represent themselves as being interactive. But the perception of what's interactive varies among learners. Therefore, be more specific and state the type of interaction, such as "hands-on exercises with simulated software" or "a simulation of an office environment."

Create a Promotional Plan

After you identify the type of material you need to promote the learning program, prepare a plan for the types of promotions you will use and when. Here is a suggested timeline:

- *Before the online learning program is available:* Prepare collateral material and make sure that it is ready for the day of announcement. Also prepare some promotional materials that will raise awareness of the program. Generate good advance support for the online learning program. One way to do so involves piloting the program with a group that is anticipated to positively respond to it. Their positive experiences will generate good word-of-mouth, which should inspire others in the organization to consider trying the program.

■ *One month to six weeks after the course is published:* Prepare another wave of promotional materials, to maintain the awareness of the course following its initial launch.

■ *When enrollment drops:* Carry out another round of promotion to rebuild awareness of the course. Ongoing publication of a catalog also helps to maintain awareness.

Finally, make sure that you leave time in your schedule to perform these activities. Some organizations devote as much as 20 percent of their resources to the marketing effort. Although that might not be feasible in every organization, failing to devote more than an hour or two to promotion could doom the online learning program to low usage and poor results.

SUPPORTING AND MAINTAINING AN ONLINE LEARNING PROGRAM

Although most people express great enthusiasm about designing and developing their first online learning program, few shriek with excitement about supporting and maintaining it. In fact, few people even think about it. Supporting and maintaining an online learning program involves the following activities:

■ scheduling technical fixes
■ providing ongoing tutoring services
■ scheduling maintenance of the technical content of the learning program
■ managing the evaluation of the learning program.

Scheduling Technical Fixes

Despite advance testing to identify programming bugs before publication of the online learning program, some will emerge under the rigor of everyday use. A technical fix refers to process of correcting these bugs. Because the bugs impede learning, they must be corrected in a timely manner.

In an ideal world, you would fix them immediately. But, in the real world, you are likely to have started a new project when bugs appear on the existing learning program. By scheduling time in advance to make inevitable fixes on one learning program as you move onto the next, you can avoid disrupting the timeline for your future learning programs.

Providing Ongoing Tutoring (E-Coaching) Services

Although you should anticipate programming bugs, you will more likely receive questions about the course content from the online learners. Some will not understand some or all of the content. Others will need help applying the content to their personal situations. Still others will seek enrichment beyond the scope of the online learning program. Tutoring—also called e-coaching—can meet the needs of these learners. E-coaching can take many forms:

- communication by email
- a toll-free number that learners can call for tutoring
- online office hours, conducted either through simple chat or instant messaging software or with more sophisticated collaboration software.

If you provide e-coaching services with your learning program, you need to plan for this by setting aside staff and time for this purpose.

Scheduling Maintenance to the Technical Content

If you know in advance that the content of the learning program is likely to change after you develop it, you should plan for that as part of maintenance. For example, if you develop an online learning program about a new product, and you know that new models or enhancements will be made available three to six months later, you should plan for that as part of the planning for course maintenance.

Generally, updates to the content fall into three categories:

- minor update, which involves changes to specific passages, usually a word or sentence here and there, an occasional paragraph, or perhaps a new or changed illustration
- medium revision, which involves the addition of new sections, as well as changes to specific passages and graphics
- major revision, which involves an overhaul, either to the visual appearance of the learning program or to the content as well (often corresponding to a complete overhaul of the product).

Medium and major revisions are, essentially, entirely new projects and should be scheduled as such.

As you plan to maintain the learning program, also leave time to maintain its content. The more you know about planned changes in advance, the better you can estimate the time needed. Otherwise, a best guess ensures that some time will be available in course developers' schedules.

Compiling and Reporting the Evaluations of the Learning Program

As part of the early phases of design, you developed a plan for evaluating the learning program. You prepared drafts of satisfaction surveys, tests, and follow-up assessments before you even decided how to format and present the content.

You should plan to administer these evaluations, and compile and report the results. Specifically, consider the following:

- *Update the evaluation instruments:* Because you wrote them before developing the content and might have made adjustments to the objectives of the learning program, the evaluations must reflect those changes to provide valid feedback.
- *Plan for administration of the evaluations:* Consider how you will solicit feedback on course satisfaction. Will you ask every student to complete a form (be aware that most won't), or will you use follow-up methods, such as randomly generated email messages and telephone calls? Consider how you will test for learning. Have you built this assessment into the course or will you administer it in person? How will you keep records? To whom will you report results? Consider how you will track long-term changes in behavior that result from the learning. How will you reach learners—by email, telephone, or some other method? Whom else will you survey?
- *Report the results:* Specifically, who will receive the evaluation results—members of the learning team or perhaps the client for whom you developed the learning program? What format will the reports take? Do different groups receive different reports? Will you compare results across courses?

CLOSING AN ONLINE LEARNING PROJECT

Last, consider how you plan to close the project. If the course goes into maintenance with no major updates planned for a while, perhaps you want to close the development part of the project. Closing the project involves two activities: conducting a postmortem and preparing a project history file.

Conducting a Postmortem

Because people learn best by experience, one of the most significant activities you can conduct after completing an online learning project is one in which the development team identifies the lessons learned that might carry into future projects. A very effective method of identifying these lessons is a special meeting of the project team called the postmortem. A postmortem is a meeting of all members of the project team at the end of the project with the purpose of:

- identifying what went well and should be repeated on future projects
- what did not go well and how to avoid these situations on future projects.

See the companion Website (http://saulcarliner.home.att.net/oll/index.html) for a more detailed suggestions on how to conduct a postmortem.

Preparing a Project History File

A project history file is a repository of all key information about the development of an online learning program. This information can be used in several different ways:

- Records of the time and cost of each completed activity can be used as tools to estimate the schedule and budget of future projects; the more you base future estimates on past performance, the more accurate your estimates will become.
- Records of proposals and needs analyses can be used as input to future projects. In some cases, the information can be reused, reducing the time needed to conduct an analysis. In others, the information serves as one of many sources of input for the project.
- Design plans can be reused, or they can serve as a framework for building designs of new learning programs (much the way that architects base designs for future outlets of franchised fast-food restaurants on previous ones).
- Lessons learned can be used to improve the overall management of a project.

Although each organization needs different information in a project file, some common elements include

- the project proposal
- report of the needs analysis
- design plans
- prototypes
- copies of each draft
- feedback from pilot tests
- copies of comments submitted for each plan and draft
- copies of the planned and actual budgets and schedules
- at least two copies of the finished learning program, as well as any accompanying material
- minutes of the postmortem meeting and other lessons learned
- names of contact people.

Your Turn

This chapter provided an overview of how to launch, support and maintain, and close your online learning project. It explained how to create a strategy for promoting the program and set realistic expectations for online learning. It also explained how to support and maintain an online learning program, through such activities as fixing programming bugs, offering e-coaching services to learners, scheduling revisions, and tracking evaluations. Last, it explained how to complete the project by conducting a postmortem and preparing a project file. Now, here is your chance to apply these concepts to your own situation.

Use the checklist in worksheet 12-1 to make sure your "launch, support, and maintain" program is on track.

Activity	Checklist
Launch	☐ Prepare a strategy for promoting the learning program. ☐ Manage expectations for the learning program. ☐ Promote the learning program through at least three avenues.
Support and Maintain	☐ Prepare fixes for programming bugs. ☐ Provide e-coaching or tutoring services. ☐ Identify known updates to the content. ☐ Compile and report results of evaluations. ☐ Set aside time for support.
Close the Project	☐ Conduct a postmortem. ☐ Prepare a project history file. Make sure that you include the project proposal, report of the needs analysis, design plans, prototypes, copies of each draft, feedback from any pilot tests, copies of comments submitted for each plan and draft, copies of the planned and actual budgets and schedules, at least two copies of the finished learning program, minutes of the postmortem meeting, and names of contact people.

Worksheet 12-1. Final steps for your e-learning program.

Now, try creating a course description for your e-learning program (worksheet 12-2).

Worksheet 12-2. Create a course description for your program using figure 12-1 as a guide.

Title:

Length: Just list the time, such as XX minutes or XX hours

About This Course: Describe the course in 50–75 words. Begin with an action verb. Do not begin with the redundant words, "This course . . ."

_____

_____

_____

_____

_____

Objectives
Main Objective:

Supporting Objectives: To achieve the main objective, you should be able to:
-
-
-
-
-
-
-
-

Who Should Attend: List job titles; this does not need to be a formal sentence.

_____

_____

Prerequisites: List the skills learners are assumed to have, and then state the course or other material where learners can develop those skills.

Skills	Course
_____	_____
_____	_____
_____	_____
_____	_____
_____	_____

References

ASTD. (2001). "Learning Circuits Glossary." www.learningcircuits.org.

Carliner, S. (1999). *An Overview of Online Learning.* Amherst, MA: HRD Press.

Carliner, S. (1998). "Business Objectives: A Key Tool for Demonstrating the Value of Technical Communication Products." *Technical Communication, 45*(3).

Carliner, S. (1995.) *Every Object Tells a Story: A Grounded Model of Design for Object-Based Learning in Museums.* Doctoral dissertation. Atlanta: Georgia State University.

Cooper, A. (1999). *The Inmates Are Running the Asylum.* Indianapolis: Sam's.

Davenport, T., and L. Prusak. (1997.) *Information Ecology: Mastering the Information and Knowledge Environment.* Oxford, UK: Oxford University Press.

Dick, W., and L. Carey. (1990). *The Systematic Design of Instruction* (3d edition). New York: HarperCollins.

Foshay, R.W. (1997, April 18). "Fourth Generation Instructional Design." International Society for Performance Improvement Conference. Anaheim, CA.

Gagne, R.M. (1985). *The Conditions of Learning and Theory of Instruction* (4th edition). New York: Holt, Rinehart and Winston.

Gustafson, K.L. (1991). *Survey of Instructional Development Models.* Syracuse, NY: ERIC Clearinghouse on Information Resources.

Hackos, J.T. (1994). *Managing Your Documentation Projects.* New York: John Wiley & Sons.

Horton, W. (2001). *Evaluating E-Learning.* Alexandria, VA: ASTD.

Kirkpatrick, D.L. (1998). *Evaluating Training Programs: The Four Levels* (2d edition). San Francisco: Berrett-Koehler.

Knowles, M.S. (1988). *The Modern Practice of Adult Education: From Pedagogy to Andragogy.* Cambridge, MA: Cambridge Books.

Mager, R. (1997a). *Measuring Instructional Results* (3d edition). Atlanta: Center for Effective Performance Press.

Mager, R. (1997b.) *Preparing Instructional Objectives: A Critical Tool in the Development of Effective Instruction* (3d edition). Atlanta: Center for Effective Performance Press.

Mantyla, K. (2001). *Blending E-Learning.* Alexandria, VA: ASTD.

Pfeiffer, W.S. (1999). *Technical Writing: A Practical Approach.* New York: Prentice-Hall.

Price, J., and L. Price. (2002.) *Hot Text: Web Writing That Works.* Indianapolis: New Riders.

Prusak, L. (1997.) *Knowledge in Organizations: Resources for the Knowledge-Based Economy.* Woburn, MA: Butterworth-Heineman.

Robinson, D., and J. Robinson. (1989). *Training for Impact.* San Francisco: Jossey-Bass.

Rowland, G. (1993). "Designing and Instructional Design." *Educational Technology Research and Development, 41*(1), 79–91.

Sproul, L., and S. Kiesler. (1992). *Connections.* Cambridge, MA: MIT Press.

Wilson, C. (1994, September 28). Presentation on Usability to the Board of the Society for Technical Communication. Boston, MA.

Wilson, C. (2001, March 8). Presentation to Advanced Technical Communication Class at Bentley College. Waltham, MA.

Wurman, R.S. (1989). "Hats (Hat Rack as a Model for the Understanding of Relationships and the Finding of Information)." *Design Quarterly, 145,* 1–32.

Additional Resources

Alred, G.J., C.T. Brusaw, and W.E. Oliu. (2000). *Handbook of Technical Writing* (6th edition). New York: St. Martin's Press.

Carliner, S. (1997). "Demonstrating the Effectiveness and Value of Technical Communication Products and Services: A Four-Level Process." *Technical Communication, 44*(3).

Driscoll, M., and L. Alexander. (2002). *Web-Based Training: Using Technology to Design Adult Learning Experiences* (2d edition). San Francisco: Jossey-Bass.

Hall, B. (1997.) *Web-Based Training Cookbook.* New York: John Wiley & Sons.

Horton, W. (2000). *Designing Web-Based Training: How to Teach Anyone Anything Anywhere Anytime.* New York: John Wiley & Sons.

Jonassen, D. (editor). (2002.) *Handbook of Research for Educational Communications and Technology: A Project of the Association for Educational Communications and Technology.* Mahwah, NJ: Lawrence Erlbaum & Associates.

Robinson, R. (2000, November). Interview in *Loop: The Journal of Interaction Design Education.* http://loop.aiga.org.

Rossett, A. (1987). *Training Needs Assessment (Techniques in Training and Performance Development Series).* Englewood Cliffs, NJ: Educational Technology Publications.

Wedman, J., and M. Tessmer. (1993). "Instructional Designers' Decisions and Priorities: A Survey of Design Practice." *Performance Improvement Quarterly, 6*(2), 43–57.

Zemke, R., and C. Lee. (1987). "How Long Does It Take?" *TRAINING, 24*(6), 75–80.

About the Author

Saul Carliner is a visiting professor in the department of English and Communication at the City University of Hong Kong. He teaches courses on content development, visual communication, performance support, and e-learning. His research focuses on the models, processes, and techniques of information design and the metrics used to assess content design and development.

He has held faculty positions at Bentley College in Waltham, Massachusetts, and the University of Minnesota, Twin Cities and has been a visiting instructor at the Pan African Institute for Development in Buea, Cameroon. Carliner began his career as a technical communicator and instructional designer at IBM, and continues to consult with industry by advising management on strategic issues in e-learning and online communication, conducting workshops, and designing e-learning programs. His clients include Berlitz, BellSouth, Georgia-Pacific, Guidant Corporation, IBM, Microsoft Corporation, SOLUTIONS, ST Microelectronics, 3M, UPS, and several state and federal government agencies.

His previous books include *Techniques for Technical Communicators* (Macmillan, 1993) and *An Overview of Online Learning* (HRD Press, 1999). Carliner is a fellow and past international president of the Society for Technical Communication and past president of the Atlanta chapter of the International Society for Performance Improvement. He holds a doctorate in instructional technology from Georgia State University, a master's degree in technical communication from the University of Minnesota, and a bachelor's degree in economics, professional writing, and public policy from Carnegie Mellon University.